NOVEL LIVING

FOR TRISTAN JAMES

NOVEL LIVING

COLLECTING, DECORATING,
AND CRAFTING WITH BOOKS

LISA OCCHIPINTI

Photography by
THAYER ALLYSON GOWDY

Photostyling by
KAREN SCHAUPETER

Illustrations by
LISA OCCHIPINTI

STC CRAFT/ A MELANIE FALICK BOOK

NILES

ZEIER

WHITE BY DESIGN

private places
judith wilson

BOOKS, BOXES AND PORTFOLIOS

STATE OF THE *Art*

THE STORY OF ART

ALWAYS IN VOGUE
EDNA WOOLMAN CHASE and ILKA CHASE

PAYNE

Little, Brown

HARPER & ROW

Stewart,
Tabori
& Chang

ID

DESIGN PRESS

MORROW

PHAIDON

Doubleday

OUT
OF THE
NIGHT

Jan Valtin

The Wave Watcher

A
SPINNER
IN THE
SUN

VAGA-
BONDS
HOUSE

BY
DON
BLANDING

REED

KAREL ČAPEK Harc a szalamandrákkal

A

Geacy
Edward

Edward John
BORROWER'S NAME

Winking G

Vintage

THE FORM OF A BOOK AS A
READABLE OBJECT HAS CHANGED
IMMENSELY WITH THE DAWN OF
DIGITAL READING. IN FACT, FOR
MANY, A BOOK IS NO LONGER A
TANGIBLE FORM AT ALL BUT A
file that is convenient, environmentally beneficial,
and efficient— yet, some might say, not a complete
substitute for an actual book. The act of reading
has altered little, but how we experience a book has
morphed fully.

    Novel Living is a hymnal to actual, physical books,
their forms and their functions. Books are symbols of
knowledge and are meant to be read, yet they are also
physically experienced; they are tactile and engage
our senses. We open a book, hold it in our hands, and
are aware of its scent, and when we read we hold it
close to our bodies, near our hearts, in fact. We cradle
books at our cores as we would an infant child. We
curl up with a good book. When partaking of a bound
book we are required to interact with it by the tender,
nearly silent turning of pages, like tucking a lock of hair
behind an ear. It is an intimacy that is grounding and a
counterpoint to the swipe of a screen.

All books, both digital and bound, allow us to learn about things we may never experience firsthand or go to places we may not otherwise reach. We can span time, going back in history or propelling ahead into the future. They provide platforms from which to experience nearly anything and therefore broaden our perspective of the world. We gain a greater understanding of humanity and therefore a deepened sense of compassion. As e-readers become more quotidian, we are apt to have fewer physical books in our lives and so the actual books we do have could be considered all the more sacred.

Books transport us not just through their stories, but through recalling where we were when we read them. Seeing the cover illustration of an actual book is as powerfully transportive as a scent that pulls you to some distant memory. I see Judy Blume's *Are You There God? It's Me, Margaret* and immediately I am in third grade again beneath a blinking sun standing in line for the school bus, that book in the pocket of my knapsack. The emotional connection to books is undeniable.

Though knowledge, data, and stories are contained in digital formats these days, their paperbound counterparts give them context. The style of the covers, the choice of font, the surface of the paper contribute to the experience of reading. The fact that these books have a physical presence and a conceptual one (with the ideas they contain) has made me an inadvertent bibliophile from birth. They are aesthetically and intellectually compelling. And the notion that these rectangles made of paper, comprised of ungirded potential, can fit in the palm of my hand and withstand decades, even centuries, never ceases to amaze me.

Many years ago while studying art in France, I visited the chateâu de Chantilly. It has an extensive historical library, and it was there that I saw the Duke du Berry's *Book of Hours* (*Très Riches Heures du Duc du Berry*), a magnificent illuminated manuscript created over the course of many years in the 1400s by several artisans. I had studied this book in reproduction, but to see it in person was truly transformative. In that moment, my notion of what books are and what they could be stretched and lengthened, and furthered my commitment to them. I find the symbiosis of text and image in illuminated manuscripts endlessly beguiling. That a book could be a painstakingly handmade, one-of-a-kind creation that is not only visually compelling but contains written information inspires my art-making processes to this day.

TWO OF MY ARTWORKS: LEFT *Sculpture* Set Free, *10 × 20 × 3" (25.5 × 51 × 7.5 cm), 2013. Book spines are cut and coated in beeswax then assembled into a wall relief sculpture.* RIGHT *Artist Book* Come As You Are, *9½ × 6" (24 × 15 cm) closed/9½ × 24" (24 × 61 cm) opened, 2014. An old book is upcycled into a livre d' artiste. Composite photos are printed onto the back sides of the book's original pages, assembled into an accordion binding, and recased in the original covers.*

As an artist, books have always informed my work even before I was aware of it, before I started using books as materials in my work. For the first twenty years of my career I was a painter who also made handmade books. Instinctively, the compositions of my paintings consisted of "pages." I would design the surface into sequential rectangles and incorporate combinations of words, typography, and images.

I moved from painting and making books to deconstructing them to create assemblages and artists' books (SEE LIVRES D' ARTISTES ON PAGE 25), which I do now in tandem with photographing books. I take obsolete, worn, or damaged books and deconstruct them, then reconstruct them into bespoke sculptures. I also photograph books, creating composites from a variety of sources, which allows me to author visual stories. I shared many of my techniques when I wrote *The Repurposed Library*, a volume devoted to transforming books into functional objects and art.

Now I have written *Novel Living* to further expound upon the virtues of physical books—of collecting them, appreciating them, living with them, and understanding how the ones we choose define us. As our culture espouses the digitalization of most reading material, books are becoming a distinct niche in and of themselves, and *Novel Living* addresses the ideas behind this.

Books are cultural objects, reflecting the times in which they were written and published, evincing the tastes, ideologies, and language of an era, making them inherently collectible. Books are barometers of the times (just look at the current bestseller list). Chapter 1, *Collecting Books,* covers how to source and budget a collection, why it is important to acquire books, and how to collect books based on content or form.

Fiction or nonfiction, books are thoughts made actual. And collecting based on a book's content reflects who you are as much as it shapes the space you collect in. An author expresses herself on the page, committing her ideas to the physical marks of words in order to share them. When you read, you are in unison beside the author listening to her in silent dialogue. You might even underline something that grips you or make a note in the margin. In this way you have connected. While content conveys attitudes and concerns, a book's form, its cover, typography, materials, and style are also part of its story. It is an indicator of the time in which it was printed and bound.

Though acquiring and reading books is a solitary practice, we connect to others through books. Liking the same genres is akin to liking the same music. Because books are creative and intellectual vessels, a common set of values is shared with others who like the same as you. And a library organizes books into a snapshot of who you are. Chapter 2, *Creating a Library*, addresses how to arrange, classify, and assemble books so that your library is a reservoir of stimulation, creativity, and plain old good design.

There is no denying the role books have as aesthetic objects; even when their covers are closed, they visually engage us. The books on our shelves—our libraries—are geometries that frame our personal histories. At different times in our lives we need certain books: a volume of Eastern poetry from college days, a finance guide to begin a business, parenting books to begin a family. As a collective, these books are a function of our lives, and in that way need to be honored, which is reason enough to organize them into a library. To live with them reminds us of who we are and where we came from. Their physicality has a significance that no digital file can compete with, allowing us to curate vignettes that capitalize on their innate characteristics. This is called *bookscaping*, which is also discussed in chapter 2.

When we engage with a book we practice creativity because we interpret what is being presented and visualize images in response. We imagine what a character might look like, we speculate on a setting. As we absorb the pages, which are outside of ourselves, they act as a portal inward. We respond to what is being presented and identify with it (or not). As much as we get lost in books, ironically, we can find ourselves in them as well and having them situated in a library invites discourse and conversation; it is a space for community.

And when a certain book no longer serves us, we can gift it. Chapter 3, *Preserving and Conserving*, speaks to gifting books, passing them along to someone who might gain from them, continuing the legacy. They might come across notes and highlighted passages you left behind, bridging a space between the two of you. Then it is read, put on their shelf, and you are remembered as the one who gave it to them.

Chapter 3 also covers the historical significance of books, their powerful role in society, and techniques for repairing books for longevity and collectability.

And for those who are not content to simply let books sit on their shelves, there is chapter 4, *Crafting with Books*. The Repurposed Projects in this chapter pick up the thread from my previous book, *The Repurposed Library*, offering step-by-step instructions for how to deconstruct and re-form books into design objects. The Digital Projects embrace the glory and duplication capabilities of technology, where we can create from books without deconstructing or altering them in any way.

In our current culture of speed, convenience, and planned obsolescence, we can trust that books as objects will not change (unless, of course, we create some of the repurposed projects in chapter 4!). Books are something we can return to again and again to nourish an idea or recapture a notion. Their sequence remains; the order of pages and chapters is reliable. Physical books are part of a meaningful life, and I hope this book is no exception. Plus we never have to recharge their batteries.

CHAPTER ONE

COLLECTING BOOKS

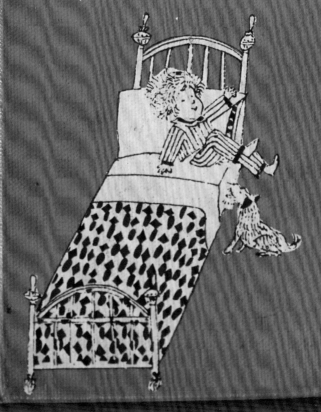

WIDE AWAKE
and Other Poems
MYRA COHN LIVINGSTON

WE ALL KNOW THE STANDARD INTERIOR DECORATING PRACTICE OF ADDING A MIRROR TO MAKE A ROOM APPEAR LARGER. BOOKS ARE MIRRORS OF A DIFFERENT KIND; THEY REFLECT OUR VALUES, OUR THOUGHTS, AND WHAT WE HOLD DEAR, ADDING ANOTHER type of breadth to a room. Though books literally (and, well . . . literally) heighten the scope and vitality of a space, they are not merely a decorative device. Likewise, a library is more than just a physical place—it is a space that tells a story. In fact, a bookshelf is readable in and of itself; as though reading a page, your eyes move along the spines as you conjure impressions. Look at friends' bookshelves and you'll get a deeper understanding of who they are and, most likely, you will see some of the same titles that you own. This chapter explores the ins and outs of collecting and sourcing books to build your own personal library, or to shape one you might have already, and how the books you choose to collect and display breathe life into your home.

LEFT *One of my prized possessions: the first book I ever bought,* Wide Awake. *I was four.*

COLLECTING

A library is a collection that is built book by book, and if you read or engage with the books you own, you most likely know your collection inside out and have a history with each volume. Every book, in its own way, has touched you, informed you—something not many inanimate objects can do. Books, no matter how many you have, create an environment of thoughtfulness because each one was acquired for its individuality and is treasured for that reason.

Beyond reading them, we collect books as aesthetic objects. Their colored, rectangular (and sometimes square) shapes are works of art. Though they are sturdy, rigid forms, they are composed of soft, supple materials: paper, cloth, glue, thread, and ink. Enjoying a book is as much a tactile experience (feeling the fabric of the cover, the edges of the pages, or an embossed signet or title) as it is a visual experience (taking in the various typography styles, illustrations, and design elements).

Though popular and convenient, e-readers tend to eliminate the tactile experience of the book, reducing it solely to its content, which is only part of what a book is. With the advent and proliferation of e-readers, I consider book collecting a form of rescuing. I fear an era in which a book is something a generation has only heard about, or seen an image of on their screens. It is up to us to safeguard books, honor them, cherish them, engage our children with them, and live with them, not as treasures so precious they are kept beneath lock and key, but as objects in daily use. In this way, they become part of our personal histories, which contributes to a broader cultural collective.

Collecting books is about gathering and adopting all that interests you, and anything that feels right in the home you continue to build, shape, and share. If you want to collect Harlequin Romance paperbacks from the 1970s and 1980s, go for it! There is no right or wrong way of going about it. But before you begin, it helps to consider what and how you collect, which will only make the hunting and gathering process richer.

Evolution of the Book

**HANDWRITTEN
SCROLL**
*first book form,
made of parchment*

CODEX
*c. AD 300–1500
covers are made
of wood, pages
are vellum*

**TYPESET
PRINTED BOOK**
*c. 1500–present
cloth and leather
covered boards,
pages are paper*

E-READER
*c. 2000–present
electronica,
no physical
materials*

The simplest way to begin a collection is to decide upon a subject and then allow it to flourish. Whatever you find intriguing, whatever interests you, is the path to follow (SEE SUBJECT IDEAS ON PAGE 18). Because books are a magnification and expansion of our inner selves, collecting is a highly personal and subjective endeavor and an extension of our personal interests. There are no rules when it comes to collecting books; in fact, the more arcane the better. And because you are physically building something—a library—book by book, it is emotionally and intellectually rewarding and viscerally satisfying. It can also become wickedly addictive—a condition called *bibliomania*, where books take over your life. But that is for another book entirely!

I bought my first book when I was four. I will never forget choosing it from a bin on a table in the downstairs, usually off-limits section of the public library where they were holding their book sale. I chose it because I liked its size and thickness, and I liked that it contained words and drawings in equal quantities. It might have cost a quarter but I would have paid a full dollar for it. Thus began my collecting.

Subject Ideas for Book Collecting

FICTION	NONFICTION	HISTORICAL PERIODS	TOPICS	MOVEMENTS
Popular novels	Artist monographs	Ancient Greece	First editions	Romanticism
Mysteries	Atlases	The Middle Ages	Leather-bound novels	Abolitionism
Literature	Biographies	The Renaissance	Livres d'artistes	Marxism
Graphic novels	Cookbooks	Civil War	Foreign language	Surrealism
Science fiction	Dictionaries	The Belle Époque	Pop-ups	Existentialism
Poetry	Fashion	The Industrial Revolution	Pulitzer Prize winners	Jungianism
Children's	Instruction manuals	The Depression	Anthologies	Women's suffrage
Westerns	Letters	American 1960s	Bestsellers	Civil Rights
Thrillers	Music			
Drama	Religion			
Erotica	Science			
	Sports			

COLLECTING FOR CONTENT

Content is subject matter. It is the words in the book, the stories, ideas, and information expressed by the author. If you're interested in content, you'll be apt to collect an author's entire oeuvre, or a grouping of, say, Caldecott Medal winners. You might build an entire collection on a particular subject area such as gardening or Beat poets or tribalism. You might have more than one copy of a title because there could be an added preface, an unabridged version, an updated edition. Or you might collect the same title in different languages. Like having a studio recording and a live version of the same album, having different versions broadens your collection and increases its merit.

As with any type of collecting, once you begin a path, it bifurcates. You might start by collecting books by nineteenth-century poets, then learn that one of the authors on your shelf also wrote novels, taking you down a whole new trail.

When content is the basis for your collecting you might ask, why pay more money for an earlier edition of the same title when you can buy a new version for less money? It is valuable to buy that earlier edition because it brings you closer to the author, nearer to the genesis of the work. Perhaps the author worked with this publisher in person, agreeing on the design or format. Perhaps the copy is signed by the author. These elements add distinction to your collection.

COLLECTING FOR FORM

Collectors have always been concerned with the book's physical beauty. Up into the eighteenth century, books were often sold unbound so customers could select personalized bindings, choosing colors and materials or incorporating a family crest. Because of this, bookbinders were often permanent workers at bookshops. It wasn't until the early nineteenth century, with the arrival of metal printing presses and mass-produced paper, that the publisher began to take responsibility for the acquiring, editing, printing, and binding as one enterprise.

A book's form is the book as a physical object, its pages and covers, the materials used in its construction (vellum, parchment, paper), the style of binding, the typography. These are also indicators of the time in which it was printed and bound, not necessarily when it was written. For instance, Shakespeare wrote in the late 1500s but his works have been published ever since. So a copy of *The Merchant of Venice* woodblock-printed on parchment and bound in hand-tooled leather covers with gilt work has a very different physical history (and obviously financial value) from that of an Oxford's World Classic copy of *The Merchant of Venice* printed twenty years ago. The content is the same, but the physical form is different. A book's binding is the historical vehicle for the content. It reflects its era of production and contributes to its value.

If you're interested in the form of the book, you might be less concerned with what they are about; reading them is ancillary. Perhaps you are drawn to collecting books with elaborately decorated spines (making for a beautiful length of shelf). Those searches might splinter into books with titles on their decorative spines, and others with *only* designs on them. You might collect leather-bound tomes. Or hand-bound letterpress-printed books. Or pulp fiction paperbacks for their swarthy cover illustrations. Or maybe you buy only red hardbacks.

I am a collector of both content and form. I mostly collect hardcover books from the twentieth century, published between 1900 and 1970, fiction and nonfiction. I like that the signatures are often stitched rather than glued. I like the cloth used to cover the boards, and any cover details, like an illustration or typographic treatment, that reflect the era of its publication. I like colophons and frontispieces, bibliophilic details that are uncommon in printed books of today. As for content, I am interested in novels, art and photography books, children's books, and biographies, though I am always looking for common books that are exceptions, like an illustrated copy of *Gone with the Wind* in German that I stumbled upon at my local library's annual book sale.

Part of my passion for book collecting is finding things within books: a note tucked into the pages, an inscription on a flyleaf, or marginalia from previous owners. For me, these are intriguing windows into the lives of people I will never meet, though we are now connected by the fact that our hands have held the same book. These are the stories beneath the ones printed on the pages, adding to the history and intimacy and, for me, the value of the book.

Must collectors read all of the books they own? Not necessarily. I am a rigorous reader—reading is one of my absolute favorite things to do—but it is impossible to read every book I collect (though I do wish I had a clone who had the time and capacity to read each and every volume). You may not have time to read all the books in your library, but each book's presence on your shelf is a totem of who you are at different times of your life.

LEFT *A midcentury German edition of* Gone with the Wind. RIGHT *Inscriptions connect us to books' previous owners.*

SOURCING

Now that you have decided on the types of books you would like to collect, the next step is to find and acquire them. Sourcing books is just as personal as determining your collection. The most obvious place to start looking is in your home. Go around your house and gather up all the books that are asunder, tucked in closets, stacked in corners, under beds, in boxes in the garage, or just settled in some heedless order. Once you bring them together you'll start to see connections between them—color, size, subject matter, author, era—that might align with your defined collections.

The real fun begins, however, with search and discovery. This might mean literally going out into the field to find books, driving to a poorly lit book barn near the sea where the books are as high as the rafters, or finding an out-of-the-way bookshop whose owner is dustier than the ancient volumes on the shelves. It is a distinct experience that is part and parcel of the practice of collecting.

Online shopping is an extraordinary tool and resource for the collector too. Not only can you locate a specific title, but you can purchase a book from anywhere in the world. There are times when I need specific books for an artwork commission and because there is a deadline, the Internet comes in very handy. Obvious places to shop online are retailing sites such as Amazon and eBay. If your searches get more specific, you may try sites that specialize in rare, collectible, and out-of-print books, or in particular subjects. Addall .com and Bookfinder.com are comprehensive sites dedicated to books, while the Antiquarian Booksellers' Association of America has a broader reach. Because the ABAA site is by and for the professional book dealer trade, it is not only great for sourcing but is also rife with collector and conservator information, plus it will give you a look into the idiosyncratic culture of book collecting.

However, I prefer sourcing in person. Whatever the book may be, I like to see it for myself and feel the materials in my hands in order to decide whether or not I want to own it. I love trawling secondhand bookstores, yard sales, thrift shops, and flea markets, and I am all about the thrill of the hunt, finding a gem at the bottom of a box at a garage sale, or amid a ragtag stack on a table at a flea market. Since negotiation is typically easier to do in person, this type of sourcing will often get you better deals—especially if you're buying several volumes—plus there are no shipping fees.

Websites for Sourcing Books for Your Collections

ABAA.org (Antiquarian Booksellers' Association of America)
A thorough site for book collecting standards, as well as a resource for book fairs, articles on collecting, and helpful FAQs.

ABEBOOKS.com
A subsidiary of Amazon since 2008, their rare and collectible arm.

ADDALL.com
An independent marketplace that searches books at forty-one online bookstores to get the best books for the best price.

ALIBRIS.com
Search the Rare and Collectible sections, and get information on condition, repair, etc.

AMAZON.com
Best for more current books. For more collectible versions, do an advanced search and click on "collectible" under condition.

BIBLIO.com
Search and purchase books globally, and locate independent bookstores anywhere in the world.

BOOKFINDER.com
An e-commerce site directly partnered with 150,000 booksellers worldwide; great for price comparisons.

COOKBOOKERY.com
Specializes in all cookbooks, especially vintage.

CRAIGSLIST.org
Always worth a gander to see what is listed in books and free.

EBAY.com
A huge flea market where you might find a gem for a steal. Always confirm the seller.

BUDGETING

Book collecting can be a highbrow, costly undertaking, but the type of collecting presented here is not so much about financial investment as it is a passionate, ongoing endeavor that serves as a testament to a life well lived, and as a preservation of books as cultural objects as we leave the analog age behind. One of the virtues of book collecting is that it is a respectable and accessible pursuit that can be done on any budget. While there are ways to determine the monetary value of books, the price or condition of a book may have no bearing on what it means to you and your collection. Some of your most cherished books might be ones that were given to you by someone you love, that originally belonged to a family member, that you purchased in a special place, or that you bought for a quarter when you were four. This is part of the subjective value of books, the individual stories they carry that only you know. For instance, I have a monograph on the painter Amadeo Modigliani that I bought at the iconic and historic Shakespeare and Company bookstore when I was a student in Paris. Every time it's in my hands I am transported back to riding the Métro, meeting up with my drawing class, and smelling baking bread at every turn. In this way, books transcend time and place.

That being said, it is no simple task to evaluate books. A friend of mine who has been a rare book dealer for thirty years described it to me as a supply/demand scenario: No matter what a book is or how beautiful it may be, if there is no market for it, it is not going to be worth as much as you might think. You'll find that most books are affordable at well under $50. Books that run beyond $100 are very rare, historically valuable books or those produced in very small editions, like livres d'artistes (SEE PAGE 25). Even within a category of, say, important first editions of literature, for example, the price range is broad: T. S. Eliot's *The Waste Land* (1922) is worth around $700, while F. Scott Fitzgerald's *The Great Gatsby* (1925) fetches around $2,700.

As you begin your hunt, set a budget that works for you. I typically do not spend more than $50 on a single book. I have no intention of re-selling the books I buy so I am not interested in profit margins or financial gain. I am investing in my personal collection. When buying books online it is easy to compare sellers' prices, and you will frequently find a wide range. Value and therefore pricing can be just as subjective as the act of collecting. The value is what the bookseller determines the price to be based upon their research on provenance and historical value (objective) and their personal assessments (subjective). So you want to be sure you're paying a fair price no matter what you are buying. For instance, I researched the pricing on a book I own and found the majority of sellers of that same title, same publication date, and in similar condition, priced it around $16, though there were three sellers who had prices between $150 and $200 for the same exact book. Subjectivity is always a part of the equation. Bottom line: Pay what you are comfortable paying.

Besides the historical importance and beauty of a book, rarity and condition are steadfast cost factors. Rarity is determined by how many copies of a particular edition exist—the fewer copies of a title in existence, the more costly it will be. As for condition, clearly, the less wear and tear a book has, the more it is worth. On page 27 are common distinctions used by booksellers, ordered from best to worst. There are also many increments sellers use to describe condition, such as *extremely fine*, *near fine*, etc. Refer to page 26 for these and other abbreviations that sellers use in their online listings.

And then there is the windfall. Once people know you are a bibliophile, they will offer you boxes and bags and bundles of books they need to let go of. Before you load the books onto your shelves, make sure to consider each one and whether it fits into your collection (or is really of any interest to you at all). A little curating can go a long way toward preventing bibliomania!

Livres d'Artistes

Livres d'artistes, French for artists' books, are deluxe-edition books made in very small quantities or sometimes only in an edition of one (called a one-off or unique book). Because they are limited editions, they are highly collectible and not something you're likely to find at a book sale. When you collect artists' books, you are acquiring art.

Livres d'artistes were incarnated in 1890s Paris, conceptualized and produced by the gallerists Ambroise Vollard and Daniel-Henry Kahnweiler to serve a middle-class market, and have become a specialized and thriving art form.

They are not simply illustrated books but collaborations between artist and writer, and oftentimes with printers, designers, binders, and dealers. Exquisitely crafted books, they incorporate fine binding and are mostly, if not always, handmade, and often employ nontraditional and/or rare materials. They are frequently letterpress-printed and bound in the form of a traditional book, but can also be conceptual and sculptural in nature and construction.

The distinction of artists' books is that they are not simply loose pages grouped together and bound into a single form; rather the entire form of the book is considered as a whole. The style of binding and the choice of materials are intentional and relate to the book's theme. Their form and content are not exclusive of each other but symbiotic.

Artist and friend Wilfredo Chiesa collaborated with a poet and a musician to create this limited-edition artist book. Relatos de un Paisaje Asesinado (Recounts of an Assassinated Landscape) *11 × 15 × 1.5" (28 × 38 × 4 cm) closed/22 × 15" (56 × 38 cm) open, 1978. Book design, art, and binding by Wilfredo Chiesa, poetry by Tomás López Ramirez, music by Rafael Aponte-Ledée.*

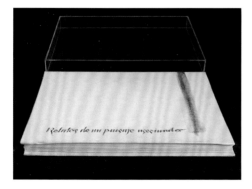

Common Descriptive Abbreviations Used by Booksellers

A.MS.	autographed manuscript	N.F.	near fine
BCC.	book club edition	O.P.	out of print
BDG.	binding	O/W	otherwise
BKPL	bookplate	P.	poor
CL.	cloth	PB	paperback
CPY.	copy	PP.	pages
CV.	cover	PL.	illustration plate
DISB.	disbound	REPRD.	repaired
D-J	dust jacket	REV.	revised
ED.	edition, editor, edited	S.C.	softcover
EDN.	edition	SGD.	signed
E.F.	extremely fine	SLPCS.	slipcase
E.P.	endpapers	STNS.	stains
F.	fine	SWD.	sewed
F/O	fold out	T.E.G.	top edges gilt
FRONT.	frontispiece	UNB.	unbound (loose pages)
FX.	foxing	V.F.	very fine
G.	good	V.G.	very good
H.C.	hardcover	WN.	worn
ILL.	illustrated, illustrations	WR.	wrapper (dust jacket)
INSCR.	inscribed, inscription		
M.	mint		
MS.	manuscript		
MSSG	missing		
N.D.	no publishing date		

Book Condition Guide

MINT

An absolute perfect copy, like new, and in the same condition as the day it was published/made; if it was issued with a dust jacket, the jacket should be without any tears, flaws, etc.

FINE

A book with no damage; in older books: only minor flaws from little usage; bindings should still be crisp; if there is a dust jacket, only small tears or stains should appear.

VERY GOOD

A book with few and minor signs of wear on either the binding or the pages, but no tears; no longer pristine but still collectible. For many collectors, this is the minimum acceptable condition. Any defects must be noted by the seller.

GOOD

A used book with all of its pages intact. It is worn yet complete and might have such infractions as highlighted text, loose bindings, a torn dust jacket, or bent corners. Any defects must be noted by the seller.

FAIR

A very worn, much-handled book with all its pages present, though endpapers or a title page may be missing. There might be markings, but they do not hinder readability. Any defects must be noted by the seller.

POOR

A book that is extremely worn but does have all of its text pages and is still readable, though it may be missing maps or illustrated pages. It may be stained, spotted, scuffed, and/or have loose bindings or pages. Any defects must be noted by the seller. Reading copies fall into this group.

READING COPY

A used book that is worn to such a degree that it is not in good enough condition to be considered collectible. Any defects must be noted by the seller.

CHAPTER TWO

CREATING A LIBRARY

VICTOR HUGO

THE TOILERS OF THE SEA

the party's over now.

john gruen

HOTEL BEMELMANS

VIKING

Pushcart

WALDEN

David Lodge *Small World*

Abbott **Flatland**   PRINCETON

e-topia   MITCHELL

The New York Times HOURS WEST COAST   TASCHEN

IMPERIAL PALACE

au 07:04   439   Feature:
                               Size and Architects in Portugal

Erwin   Wurm   Wear   Me   Out

Photograph

IN ITS SIMPLEST DESCRIPTION A LIBRARY IS A SPACE DEVOTED TO HOUSING BOOKS SO THAT THEY ARE EASILY ACCESSIBLE TO US.

When we amass books and cobble them into a collection, we create a context wherein each book relates to the others on the shelf. No matter what your space limitations or your aesthetic sensibilities, a library is a place that invites discourse and thoughtful interaction (whether you are discussing shelf content or not).

Best of all, a library silently states that this is a zone dedicated to unwinding and restoring oneself. I prefer a library to be an unplugged sanctuary where one can be disconnected from online distractions. Most of our lives are spent being friended, poked, tagged, and tracked. A library is a space that allows us to be grounded by the tactile nature of our reading material (i.e., full sentences inked on paper versus the abbreviated directives of a text message). A library is a space for partaking in the therapeutic nature of books, which encourage us to contemplate and go inward.

The concept of a personal library has evolved from a formal, sequestered chamber to an interactive space that doesn't necessarily need to be contained to a single room. It can be an area, a corner, a niche. Whatever its size and affectations, it is ultimately about creating a personal sanctuary for you and your books, and all that it requires is some shelving, seating, and lighting.

If your books live in more than one room of your home, try curating them by room. Cookbooks, of course, suit the kitchen, but consider aligning them also along the dining room's sideboard, or arranging them as a centerpiece (SEE PAGE 39). Picture books and pop-up books in the living room are ideal for perusing and starting conversations. You might keep books from your childhood on a hanging shelf in an intimate corner of your bedroom (SEE LIGHTED BOOK BOX ON PAGE 44). Or when guests visit from out of town, you might create a hanging selection of regional books for them, like sightseeing or hiking guides, books on local history, or even fiction that takes place in your neck of the woods (SEE SLING BOOKS ON PAGE 54).

SHELVING

Because books have a distinct and indelible presence in a room, their placement deserves the same thought and consideration you would give to hanging artwork or arranging furniture. When planning out your shelving, consider the vertical height between shelves, the depth of each shelf, and the weight, size, and number of books in your collection. This equation determines what kinds of shelves will work best for what you own. For instance, a collection of novels will fit on slender and thinner shelves while a grouping of photography books will require wider and thicker shelves to support their weight. Following you will find a brief overview of shelving options and other traditional library furniture, which will help you make the right decision about how to shelve your books.

OPPOSITE
A freestanding bookcase makes a smart room divider.

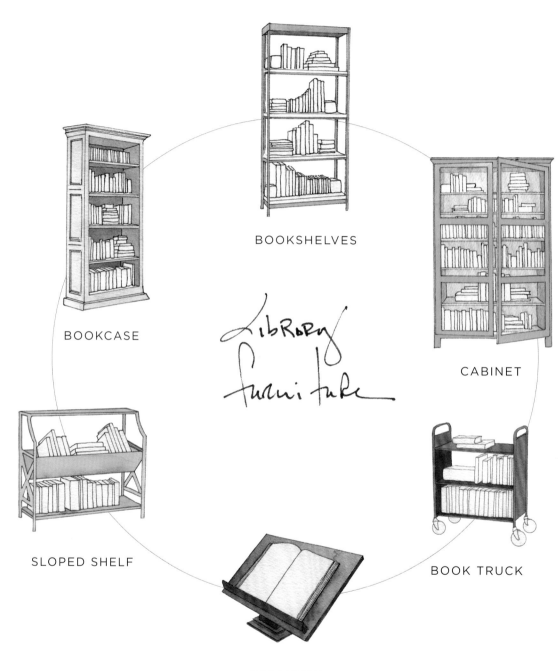

BOOKSHELVES

BOOKCASE

CABINET

Library furniture

SLOPED SHELF

BOOK TRUCK

TABLETOP
LECTERN

* *Bookcases* Either freestanding or built-in, bookcases are shelving units that have sidewalls, and sometimes backs. Books arranged in bookcases have the advantage of the sidewalls to give them support. And because of that, a freestanding bookcase can make an ideal room divider.

* *Bookshelves* Similar to bookcases, bookshelves can also be freestanding. But because they do not have sidewalls they require bookends (SEE THE TEXTILE BOOKENDS ON PAGE 58 TO MAKE YOUR OWN). You can also use horizontal stacks of books to keep vertical books upright and in place. There are also wall-hung bookshelves that can line an entire wall, end to end, top to bottom, or may also be in the form of a small shelf unit acting as an altar for select books. If you are short on space, an ideal design tack is installing wall shelves above windows and/or doorways around the perimeter of a room. Books are quietly perched above you while you reside beneath them.

* *Glass-Fronted Cabinets* These have interior shelves and are another way to store your books while also showcasing them. The closed doors will keep your collections dust-free. Consider using curio cabinets and china cupboards.

* *Book Trucks* These wheeled carts are typically used by libraries and schools. They are pure function and highly durable, and add an unexpected bit of industrial-strength style to a home setting. Available from library suppliers, they come in wood and a range of bold colors if you opt for the metal versions (SEE RESOURCES ON PAGE 138).

* *Tabletop Lecterns* Common in libraries, a lectern holds a book at just the right angle for display. A book that is referenced often, such as the *Oxford English Dictionary*, could be left open for quick perusal.

* *Sloped Shelves* This is another traditional library piece, which holds books securely by cradling them, fore-edge first, at a 45-degree angle, ensuring little strain on their spines and making it easy to read titles.

* *Ladder Shelves* (SEE PAGE 66) For an inventive shelf solution, upcycle an old ladder into a freestanding shelving unit. Not only simple in design, but quick in execution, you can fabricate sturdy and sizable book storage in no time. Ladder shelves are also highly transportable if you move a lot.

Shelving Do's & Don'ts

Shelving is not only a noun but a verb, and for bibliophiles there is an etiquette to this practice. First and foremost, do not shelve books too tightly. You should be able to slide a book out of its place easily and without pulling out the books beside it. When the shelf is filled, remove two or three books: This is the fullest you want your shelf to be. You also want to have room to add to your collection.

Avoid placing books horizontally on top of the vertically stacked books. Putting books on top of upright books can cause damage and look cluttered. Books are best stored either vertically standing or horizontally stacked on the shelf to prevent damage to their forms.

ORDERING AND ORGANIZING

Books that are simply stacked and stored on shelves do not make a library. Books become a library when they are curated and organized. The shelf is a stage for your books, and their order is how they perform; it is their choreography. Following are some ideas for organizing your collections.

Bibliographic Order

Part of shelving etiquette is organizing your books so you can find each one easily. One of the most fundamental ways of arranging books is in bibliographic order: grouping them first by subject, then within that group alphabetizing them by either the author's last name, the title, or a subsection of the subject. For instance, if you have a collection of craft books, you might group the books on needlework separately from the books on collage and bookbinding. Then, within each of those subsections, you might alphabetize the books by the author's last name.

Size or Color

An entirely different approach is to organize books by their physical forms: size or color. When shelving by size, you want the largest and heaviest books on the bottommost shelves to prevent shelves from sagging and for safety's sake (a falling book is a concussive book!). To also prevent shelf sag, lighten the center of your shelves with smaller books or stack a few books horizontally between upright ones to mitigate the load. You can also use this method to design with your books: Create combinations of uniform vertical and horizontal stacks to form a bookish landscape.

ABOVE *Stack books horizontally and vertically for spacing and for visual interest.*

Grouping books by color might not make it as easy to find a specific title but is visually dramatic. Entire shelves comprised of variegated color are like bands of paint. Full shelves of hues make a statement. This is how I shelve my vintage and collectible books since their form is more important to me than their content.

Color Coding

If you want to alleviate the needle-in-a-haystack-ness that is part of the color- or size-based system of arrangement, merge aesthetics with function by covering your books in color-coded paper and writing their titles on the spines. For example, novels might be covered in white paper, poetry in red, literature in brown. Color-coded book jackets are also ideal for a family that shares shelving space: Each family member can have a signature book jacket color. In the mid-twentieth century, Penguin Paperbacks published a series of literature using color-coded covers (for instance, orange was for fiction and green was for crime), and these have since become highly collectible.

Creating a thematic tableau
of books on top of a dresser.

BOOKSCAPING

Another way to arrange books is to design with them, which I like to call "creating a bookscape." Look around your home and ask yourself where a landscape of books might logically and effortlessly add color, texture, and thematic depth. Tucked-away and odd-shaped spaces make ideal nesting spots for a flock of books. For instance, you might want to assemble books in a nonoperative fireplace, align them along kitchen soffits, or stack them on an accent chair in a corner. Be cautious of a cluttered approach, however—you want to be deliberate and make a single, clean shape that suits the space where you place them. For instance, over my kitchen stove is a space intended for a microwave (which I prefer hidden in a cabinet) and I have stacked several vintage cookbooks there, mixed in with glassware, a creamer and sugar bowl, a salt shaker, and glass beakers. I am a proponent of using the things you have, taking good care of them, but not sequestering them into stasis. Live with books as part of your everyday life.

Books with illustrated covers or compelling design, and of course artist books (or livres d'artistes) are obvious books to design with, but I say all books are aesthetically viable. A grouping of mystery titles, their spines aligned, forms a poem of sorts; a body of books set on a shelf is an installation. Once you start

Placing books in idle spaces enlivens them and gives them purpose.

to look at books in this new light, there are myriad ways to incorporate them into your living and working spaces that are meaningful and expressive of who you are. Below are three simple ways to create bookish landscapes.

Tableau

Using as few as three or as many as seven books that relate to one another, either by color, size, or theme, arrange the books on a surface such as a dresser, nightstand, or kitchen counter—a place where they are seen but not in the way of activity. Then, add a few objects to the arrangement that coordinate with the theme. No need to go out and shop—hunt around your home, office, or yard for items you already have.

For instance *Water Babies, A Gift from the Sea, Four Seas to Dreamland, The Book of Sailing Knots,* and Jacques Cousteau's *The Silent World* make a well-edited and compelling oceanic story when grouped together. Arrange them with simple objects like seashells, beach stones, sea glass, and a jar filled with sand. Get extra crafty and put a message in a bottle. This can be an ongoing exhibition— great to do with kids and a lovely touch in the guest room.

Centerpiece

As an unexpected and totally functional dinner table centerpiece, books rank high. Create three stacks of books at varying heights in the middle of your table. Cookbooks, restaurant guides, and books on wine are obvious choices, but consider the food you're serving and who your guests are and you may find other ideas. Then place candles, little jars of flowers, salt and pepper shakers, and any other odds and ends atop the stacks. Add handmade bookmarks as place-setting tags that your guests can take home.

LEFT
Thoreau's
Walden *joins
landscape
and garden-
ing books
to make an
outdoor table
setting more
thoughtful.
Bookmark
place-setting
tags are in
the fore-
ground.*

RIGHT
*Photography
books with
bold, color-
coordinated
covers make
a statement
on a ledge.*

Wall Art

For instant graphic art, install a simple picture ledge on a wall in an otherwise
inactive spot and place books with their covers facing outward. Circulate your
collections by changing out the featured books to suit holidays, celebrations, or
seasons, or anything that sparks your imagination. A stairway, hall, foyer, or that
odd nook that nothing seems to fit in are places where books and their covers can
create a setting.

THINNING OUT

A library is a living thing, always evolving, growing, and shedding, only to expand
again. Thinning out is a necessary part of collecting books and maintaining a
library. Sometimes you need to thin out your shelves because you are moving or
moving in with someone and combining libraries. Just like your closet should
be cleaned out once or twice a year, your library shelves deserve the same. Purge
the books that no longer serve you, starting with outdated travel guides, self-help
books, old college textbooks, or mass-market versions of quality literature. When

merging collections, begin with duplicate titles, keeping the more valuable ones. Give these flagged books to friends or family, or donate them to local libraries or to schools and churches for fund-raising books sales (SEE MORE ON GIFTING IN CHAPTER 3). It is often a tough decision to oust a book, especially a lovely and thoughtful one, so passing it along to a person or organization you know will enjoy it (or needs it) is fitting. This is part of how books connect us to others.

Doubtlessly you have read a book (or two, or ten) that has moved you, and these are great to give away because you are not only giving the physical book, but also bestowing the experience that awaits within it. In this way, I believe, books are the only acceptable re-gift item (ever!). Many years ago, my sister gave me an illustrated book on fairies and when I was thinning out my shelves, I decided to give it back to her since, at the time, she was pregnant with my niece. Now it is on my niece's bookshelf and we read it together when I visit.

Another option for these purged books, particularly the ones whose value may not be what it once was, is to give them new life by making art with them or crafting them into functional objects (SEE PAGES 100–121).

CATALOGUING

No bibliophile is worth her salt if she doesn't know what she has. Like adding a little vermouth to your soup stock, cataloguing a personal library is not necessary but creates a layer of refinement. Whether you go old school and use a card catalog system or create a digital filing system, cataloguing your books is a worthwhile enterprise to the dedicated collector. In addition to general information, you can annotate each entry with pertinent details, such as how you acquired the book or any inscriptions.

I use library borrower cards alphabetized in two wooden boxes to catalog my books (SEE PAGE 42). One box is labeled "reading" for the more current books that I read, use, and reference, and the other is "vintage" for my collectible books. Within these two groups I separate them into subsections of "fiction" and "nonfiction." If digital cataloguing is more your style, create a spreadsheet on your computer. There are also many apps for book cataloguing like iBookshelf and Book Crawler.

D

A

Gorey
Edward

AUTHOR
Amphigorey
15 books by Edward Gorey
DATE DUE   BORROWER'S NAME
Berkley Publishing Group
New York   1972

8"×11"   pp   softcover

Vintage

Reading

B

AUTHOR
Basic Typography
TITLE
a design manual
DATE DUE
Watson-Guptill
New York
8½"×11"   pp 192   so

Top Notch Teacher Products,

C

Delaney
Barbara

AUTHOR
The Cloth Paper Scissors Book
TITLE

DATE DUE   BORROWER'S NAME

Interweave
Loveland CO   2011

8"2×10"4" pp 160   softcover

p106-09 my chapter
"Character Study"

Top NOVEL LIVING

A

Rothenstein

Old School Card Catalog

MATERIALS

Library borrower cards

Wooden or metal box no smaller than
3½ w × 4 ½ d × 8" l (9 × 11 × 20 cm)
(an old thin drawer is perfect for this)

Heavy-stock paper cut into twenty-six 3½ × 5"
(9 × 12 cm) pieces for alphabetized dividers

Metal bookplates (adhesive ones are best) with
paper inserts

TOOLS

Pencil and metal ruler

Craft knife

1 Affix the bookplate to the front
of your box and cut a piece of the
paper to fit its slot, then label
the paper fiction, nonfiction,
collectible, or simply ex libris . . .
("from the library of . . . ").

2 Mark the dividers with each letter
and alphabetize them in the box.

3 Write your entry for each book on
the library borrower cards, using
the standard format for book
cataloguing:

> *Author name last, first.*
> *Title.*
> *Publisher, place published,*
> *date.*
> *Size of book.*
> *Number of pages.*
> *Any illustrations.*
> *Annotations [optional]*

4 File accordingly.

*Boxes and
borrower cards
let you be your
own librarian.*

Lighted Book Box

This is simple and elegant book storage that doesn't take up any floor space. Basic wooden crates, whether purchased new or sourced from a flea market, are outfitted with a little mood lighting and textile or wallpaper design, then hung on the wall. I made mine from wooden wine crates and vintage wallpaper. The little light inside illuminates the books like art.

Wooden crate (no smaller than 10 × 12 × 5" /
   25 × 30.5 × 12 cm) (you can also
   use old dresser drawers)

Wallpaper (or fabric)

One sheet of ¼" (6 mm) thick
   foam core

Acrylic paint, to match wallpaper
   or fabric choice

Wireless puck light

Two screws with wall anchors

Spray glue

Power drill with appropriate drill bit to fit screws

Sandpaper

Paintbrush

Pencil and metal ruler

Craft knife

Bone folder

Hot glue gun and glue sticks

1 Decide whether you want your book box to be oriented vertically or horizontally. Consider the books it will hold and where you are placing it on the wall.

   Drill two holes that fit the size of your screws on the back of the crate about one third of the way down from the top and equally spaced apart. Sand any rough edges or nicks on your crate.

2 Paint the outer facing edges of the crate with the acrylic paint. Allow to dry.

LEFT *A puck light illuminates the stacks within.*

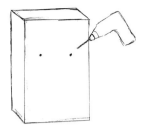

1   DRILL TWO HOLES ON BACK OF
CRATE. SAND ROUGH EDGES

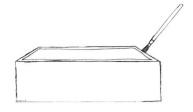

2   PAINT OUTER FACING EDGES

FOAM CORE

trim corners

3   GLUE WALLPAPER OR FABRIC TO FOAM CORE

center

4   CENTER AND AFFIX PUCK
LIGHT TO CRATE CEILING

3 Measure the height and width of the back wall of the crate, reducing the measurement by ⅛" (3 mm) on the top and one side, and cut your foam core to fit to that measurement.

4 Cover the foam core with your wallpaper. Apply spray glue to the foam core, and place it glue side down on the back of the wallpaper. Flip over and smooth out any wrinkles or bubbles with the bone folder. Flip back over, trim your corners for a nice finish, and wrap and glue the edges.

Affix the covered foam core to the back of the crate with hot glue.

5 Measure the center point of the crate's "ceiling" and affix your puck light at that point, following the package instructions.

6 Position the crate on the wall where you would like it to hang and use a pencil to mark where the screws will go, measuring the space between the two holes.

Set the screws and wall anchors in the wall at the points you marked, with the screws extending out ⅜" (1 cm), and hang the crate from the holes drilled in the back of the crate.

Paperback Rider

For this project, a lazy Susan is retrofitted into an organizing carousel to hold the books you're in the middle of reading, the ones you're going to get to next, and the ones from which you just need a daily fix. With its four sections, it is also great for a family of readers, with each person having their own quad in which to place their books.

Wooden lazy Susan
(approximately 15" [38 cm] diameter)

One 6 w × ¾ d × 14" l
(15 × 2 × 35.5 cm) pine board

Two 6 w × ¾ d × 6½" l
(15 × 2 × 16.5 cm) pine boards

Four 1" (2.5 cm) long #8 screws

Four 12" (30.5 cm) square sheets
patterned paper

Clear wood varnish

Decorative drawer pull

Masking tape

Pencil and ruler/T-square

Power drill and ⁵⁄₃₂" (4 mm) drill bit

Sandpaper

White glue and brush

Bone folder

Craft knife

Liquid Nails

Screwdriver

1 Turn the lazy Susan over and use masking tape to tape the spinning wheel in place so it doesn't turn while you're working. Turn the lazy Susan back over and use a pencil to mark an X on the circle, using a ruler or T-square to get perfect 90-degree angles.

Measure in 3" (7.5 cm) from the edge of the circle along the four drawn lines and mark these spots. Drill a hole at each of these four marks.

2 Sand and varnish the edges of the three pine boards. Use at least two coats of varnish for a nice finished look.

3 When completely dry, cover the sides of the boards with your patterned paper. Decide upon the placement of your patterns so that when you assemble the finished carousel, the correct patterns are adjacent to one another. Cut each piece of paper ½" (12 mm) larger than the board on all sides. With the brush, sparingly apply white glue to the paper's back side. Place the board on top of the glued paper, flip it over, and smooth it out with your bone folder, burnishing the edges so they are secure and won't lift. Once dry, trim the extra paper with the craft knife.

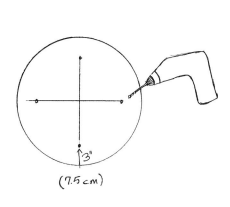

1   MARK 90-DEGREE ANGLE AND DRILL
     FOUR HOLES ON LAZY SUSAN FRONT

2   SAND AND VARNISH EDGES OF THREE
     PINE BOARDS

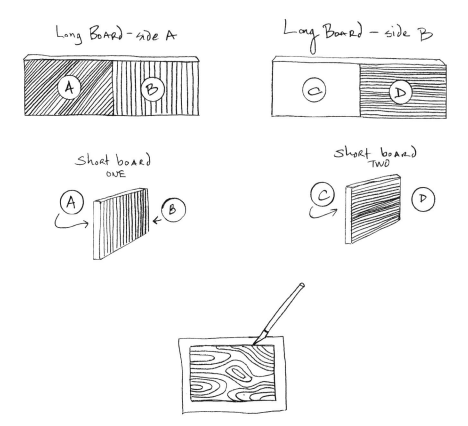

Long BOARD - side A

Long BOARD - side B

Short boARD
ONE

Short boARD
TWO

3   BRUSH GLUE ONTO PATTERNED PAPER AND ADHERE TO BOARDS.
     TRIM OVERHANG WITH CRAFT KNIFE

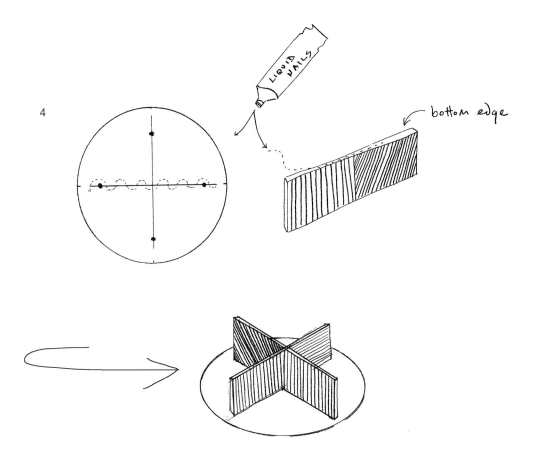

4   ATTACH BOARDS TO LAZY SUSAN WITH
       LIQUID NAILS, ALIGNING PATTERNS

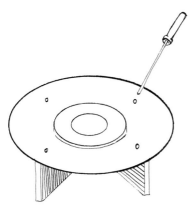

5   REINFORCE WALLS WITH SCREWS

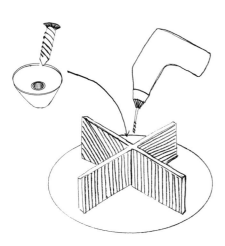

6   DRILL HOLE IN CENTER AND ATTACH
DRAWER PULL

4 Assemble the carousel. Run a sparing amount of Liquid Nails along one arm of the X you drew, then do the same along the bottom edge of the 14" (35.5 cm) long covered board. Place it squarely along the line of Liquid Nails. Do the same with the two smaller boards, aligning them at right angles along the drawn lines, and being sure the patterns are in the proper place. Allow to set overnight.

5 Turn the form over and reinforce the glued walls by inserting the screws with a screwdriver.

6 Turn right side up. Mark and drill a small hole in the center X where the walls meet to attach the drawer pull that will be the turning knob. Remove the masking tape from the spinner underneath.

Sling Books

Sling books make a thoughtful visual statement and invite perusing. I came up with this idea when I was hosting out-of-town guests. Now I regularly put out books on subjects or authors my guests might like, ideas I want to share, or books of local interest. Having them out and hanging around rather than stacked up presents the chosen books in an unorthodox way and adds an element of design to the room. This is also adorable in a nursery.

24" (55 cm) long towel bar, plus screws
to install (you can also make a hanging
bar with an iron pipe, elbows, and flange)

1" (2.5 cm) wide cotton twill tape (1 yard / 1 m per
paperback or 1½ yards / 1.5 m per hardcover)

3 to 5 S-hooks

3 to 5 books

Ruler

Scissors

Power drill with appropriate drill bit
to fit screws

1 Knot the ends of the twill tape
together. Then make another knot
3 to 4" (7.5 to 10 cm) below the
first one.

2 Open the book about midway
through and slip one side of the
twill tape loop through the book,
snugly setting it into the book's
inside gutter. On the bottom outer
edge of the spine, straighten the
twill tape so the book is secure in
its sling.

3 Install the towel bar according to
the manufacturer's instructions
(or construct your own bar from
an iron pipe, elbows, and flange).
Slip an S-hook through the top
loop of twill between the knots
and hang each book from the bar.

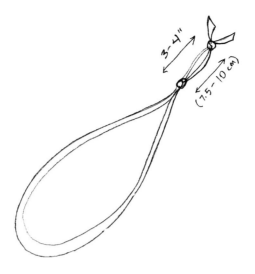

1   CREATE TWO KNOTS AT ENDS OF TWILL TAPE

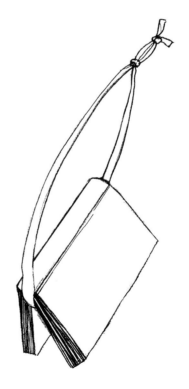

2   SLIP TWILL TAPE LOOP THROUGH BOOK CENTER AND HANG

Textile Bookends

These supple bookends are reminiscent of a child's ABC blocks. Made with fabric and filled with sand, they are a nice caesura of texture, color, and pattern along a shelf of books. They also stack well to keep larger books in place. Be sure to use upholstery or other heavyweight fabrics, like jacquard, for good form.

Lïlïan Bassman

MATTHEW ROLSTON

William Eggleston

Los Alamos

PALM SPRINGS MODERN

ARCHITECTURAL DRAWING

BROWN

CYGELMAN ROSA GLORIA

PATEN ROGNESS

HAMPTONS

Bulfinch

BULFINCH

SCALO

R

ASSOULINE

MATERIALS

¼ yard (¼ m) each of two coordinating fabrics (A and B)

5 pounds (2.25 kg) of sand per bookend

TOOLS

Sewing machine and thread

Bone folder

Pencil and metal ruler

Needle and thread

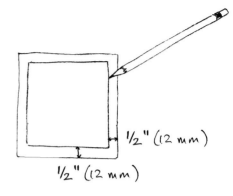

1   CUT SIX FABRIC SQUARES AND MARK
SEAM ALLOWANCES

1 Cut three 5" (12 cm) squares of fabric A and three of fabric B. Measure and mark a ½" (12 mm) seam allowance on the wrong side of each square with a pencil.

2 Lay out your squares following illustration 2 for assembly order.

3 Stitch the panels: When you sew the panels together, it is very important to start and stop your stitching ½" (12 mm) from the fabric's edge, right at your seam allowance line, in order to make cleanly squared corners.

With right sides together, stitch the squares together in this order, following illustration 2: 1 to 2 / 3 to 2 / 4 to 2 / 5 to 2 / 6 to 5.

4 Construct the cube: Stitch edges 1 and 3 together, then edges 4 and 3. You'll see the cube begin to form. Then stitch edges 5 and 1, and 5 and 4. Next, stitch panel 6, but stitch only two of the three sides, leaving one seam open for filling the cube with sand.

5 Turn the cube right side out, pushing out the corners with a bone folder (or pencil).

6 Fill the bookend with sand. Hand-stitch the seam closed.

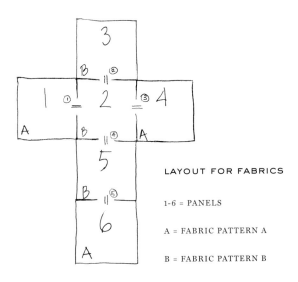

LAYOUT FOR FABRICS

1-6 = PANELS

A = FABRIC PATTERN A

B = FABRIC PATTERN B

2   LAY OUT FABRIC SQUARES AND STITCH PANELS

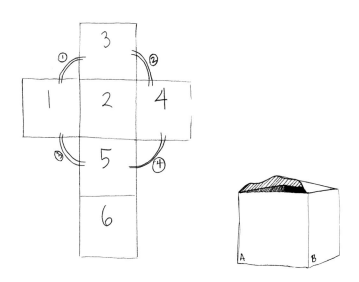

3   STITCH EDGES TO CONSTRUCT CUBE,
    LEAVING ONE OPEN SEAM FOR FILLING

Gallery Table

This table design is based on museum furniture for exhibiting books and other ephemera. This version combines the function of an occasional table with a display case. Showcase some of your favorite books, or create an interesting grouping that can be seen beneath the cheese plate. Just about any size wood table will do, so consider upcycling something in the attic, or, as I did, use an IKEA Lack table, which has a clean and simple form.

Table (SEE NOTE)

¼" (6mm) thick tabletop glass (order
from a supplier): 22 × 22" (55 × 55
cm) with holes drilled in the corners

19" (48 cm) square × ⅛" (3 mm) thick
lauan board

1 yard (1 m) of ecru linen

Four 1 × 1 × 2" (2.5 × 2.5 × 5 cm) pieces
of wood for spacers

Acrylic paint to match your
table color

One 9 × 12" (23 × 30 cm) square of felt
to match your table color

Four screws to fit holes in glass

Sandpaper

Paintbrush

Scissors

Hot glue gun and glue sticks

Liquid Nails

Pencil and metal ruler

Power drill with appropriate drill bit to
fit screws

Screwdriver

1   SAND AND PAINT SPACERS AND CUT FELT SQUARES

NOTE: *All measurements are
based upon a 22 × 22" (55 × 55
cm) IKEA Lack table, which is
the type of table I used.*

2   GLUE LINEN TO LAUAN BOARD AND TRIM EDGES

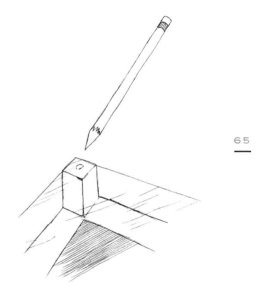

1 Assemble the table following the manufacturer's instructions. Sand and paint the wood spacers. Cut four 1" (2.5 cm) squares from the felt.

2 Cover the lauan board with the linen. Cut the linen to a 24" (60 cm) square. Place the lauan board on top of the linen and tightly wrap the edges—pulling taut—around as you set with hot glue. Trim the corners as shown and finish the edges.

3 Attach the spacers to each corner of the tabletop with Liquid Nails. Then glue the linen-covered board in the center with Liquid Nails. Allow all to set overnight.

4 Place the glass on top of the spacers and mark through the holes onto the spacers with a pencil. Set the glass aside and drill holes into the spacers. Hot glue each felt square atop a spacer and poke through the felt to expose the hole you drilled. Place the glass back on top of the spacers and attach with the screws using a screwdriver. Slip your book grouping beneath the glass.

4   MARK GLASS HOLE PLACEMENT
ONTO SPACERS. REPLACE GLASS
AND SCREW TO TABLETOP

Ladder Shelves

For those of us who want a basic book-shelf unit that is not the standard snap-together-with-an-Allen-wrench variety, ladder shelves are a great alternative. Freestanding, easy to assemble, and highly transportable, ladder shelves can be made from a ladder of any height that works for your space (preferably an old wooden one) and some wood planks.

MATERIALS

Ladder (wooden is best)

Wood planks (beech or poplar are sturdy
and won't warp), ¾" (2 cm) thick

Wood screws, 1½ to 2" (4 to 5 cm) long

Bookends (optional)

Task light (optional)

TOOLS

Power saw (jigsaw or circular saw), optional

Power drill with appropriate drill bit
to fit the screws

1 Open the ladder and measure the distance between the lowest/widest rungs and add 12" (30.5 cm). This will be the width of your shelves.

2 Measure the width of the ladder and subtract 1" (2.5 cm). This is the depth of your shelves.

3 Count the number of steps. This is the number of shelves/wood planks you will need.

4 Cut your wood planking to your specifications (or have the planks cut to size at a lumberyard).

5 Position the ladder against the wall where you'd like to display your books, with the rungs perpendicular to the wall. Slip the wood planking over each level of rung, starting at the bottom.

6 If you are using a wooden ladder, tack the boards to the rungs with screws, drilling a hole through the rung and into the board, then inserting the screw.

7 Organize your books, stacking some horizontally to distribute the weight, and placing the heaviest books on the bottom. Don't forget to use bookends (SEE PAGE 58) to keep the books standing. Consider adding a task lamp at the very top.

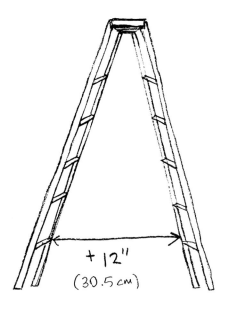

1   MEASURE RUNG DISTANCE AND ADD 12" (30.5 CM)
TO CALCULATE SHELF WIDTH

2   MEASURE RUNG WIDTH AND SUBTRACT 1" (2.5 CM)
TO CALCULATE SHELF DEPTH

CHAPTER THREE

PRESERVING AND CONSERVING

RECYCLING BOOKS OR CRAFTING
WITH THEM ARE BOTH WORTHY
OPTIONS WHEN BOOKS ARE
DAMAGED OR SHOWING SIGNS OF
A LONG, WELL-READ LIFE,
but a book weighted with significance should be
preserved or repaired to extend its tutelage and impact.
Books are powerful cultural objects because they
contain stories, accounts, and records that ensure the
legacy of a civilization. As believers in the importance
of books, we know that they are full of knowledge,
and if knowledge is power, then books are powerful.
To preserve books is to maintain them so their power
endures.

Books have historically incited controversy and, at times, have been banned and burned for the ideologies contained in them. Because of their innate power, books can be viewed as a threat by volatile and restrictive societies. In 1930s Soviet Russia, the state, fearing foreign influences on Communist culture, forced private publishers who printed translations of multinational literature to close their doors. And beginning in 1933, Nazis burned nearly 25,000 books deemed "un-German," including works by Bertolt Brecht, Karl Marx, Ernest Hemingway, Jack London, Thomas Mann, and Helen Keller.

In the United States throughout the 1920s, the United States Postal Service confiscated and burned copies of James Joyce's *Ulysses* because of indecency allegations, and the book was ultimately prosecuted and banned. Joyce was unable to publish it on U.S. soil, so Sylvia Beach, owner of Shakespeare and Company in Paris, published it in her shop in 1922. D. H. Lawrence's *Lady Chatterly's Lover* (1928) and Allen Ginsberg's *Howl and Other Poems* (1956) were also banned for obscenity. Booksellers who sold these books were arrested and jailed. Though few of us would find them offensive now, at the time they challenged the prevailing mores.

More recently, Salman Rushdie's *The Satanic Verses* (1988), believed to be heretical to Islam, was not only banned in India but also burned in the UK. Furthermore, Rushdie's life was under ceaseless threat, compelling him to live in hiding for more than a decade. Translators of the book in Italy, Turkey, and Japan were brutally attacked—some were even murdered.

In the modern era, we can maintain content via e-books, though digital forms can be deleted, altered, or hacked. They are public and can be accessed online. A book on your shelf, however, is tangible, finite, and yours alone, and keeping it is the surest way to preserve its power.

SUITABLE ENVIRONMENT

To preserve is to protect. The sole act of rescuing and collecting books while building your library is one of preservation in and of itself. A library is a sanctuary not only for ourselves, but also for our books and their ideas—a place where they are housed and safeguarded, shelved and organized, tended and regarded. Obvious measures to ensure this, like employing shelf etiquette, cataloguing, and keeping our books in optimal environments, are the basis of preservation.

One illustrious example of bibliophilic devotion is the Getty Library in Buckinghamshire, England. Built in 1991 by billionaire John Paul Getty, it houses a spellbinding collection of illuminated manuscripts and very early printed books as well as drawings and rare bookbindings. Of immeasurable value, it is protected from fire by an extinguishing system that, instead of releasing water, which would damage the books, releases argonite gas, which suffocates fire by depriving it of oxygen but will leave no residue and won't harm the books. While such state-of-the-art systems might not be as fitting for your own library, there are some preservation fundamentals that can be easily applied to protect your books.

The environment in which you store your books is vital to their well-being. Books printed on paper have survived in good condition for more than five hundred years without any special settings or devices. Basically, your books will be comfortable wherever *you* are comfortable, which means a stable climate with low humidity (40 to 50 percent) and a temperature between 55° and 75°F (130° and 165°C). If the air is too dry, pages can become brittle, and if it is too damp, mold and warping can occur. If you must store your books, house them in temperature-controlled storage units only, and keep them out of the attic or cellar.

You might, however, come across books that have resided in less than ideal habitats, contributing to age-related paper deterioration. Foxing and browning are two common afflictions that blemish pages. These occur mostly in books printed from the 1850s to the 1950s, when paper was just beginning to be mass-produced. Though the direct correlation between mass-produced paper and its deterioration is unclear, it is surmised that particles used in this early form of inexpensive paper production react with environmental factors and cause this discoloration.

Foxing—rust-toned or coffee-colored dots that appear on pages—is thought to be the result of the oxidation of flecks of metals that got into the paper pulp when it was made. Though it does not impact the integrity of the paper, foxing does decrease the book's value. It can be remedied with special bleaching treatments (done by book conservators mostly), though this impairs the strength of the page. If you acquire a book with foxing, simply accept it and be sure to shelve it in a cool, dry place to discourage further spotting.

Browning, thought to be due to acids in the paper, is an all-over page discoloration where the paper darkens and can also become brittle. Sometimes the entire book will be affected, or sometimes it only afflicts a particular signature. There is no way of reversing or repairing this type of damage. The only ministration is to store it in a cool, dry place to discourage any additional damage.

Besides poor environmental conditions, water is another enemy of books. Dampness can warp pages and covers and create mold, most often found along the outer edges of a book. If you have a moldy book, simply brush it off with a stiff-bristled brush and place it in a dry place for a few days to kill the spores.

If a book should get saturated (knocked into a pool, say, or drenched by a cup of tea), dry it out immediately by standing it upright and placing paper towels between the pages. Put it by a fan, a breezy window, or outside on a dry sunny day. When it is almost dry—feels slightly cool to the touch—close the book and weight it with other books (or anything heavy) and let it dry completely. Paperback books can be pinned to a clothesline to allow air to permeate them.

Books with foxing, browning, or water damage have lesser value and therefore can make ideal candidates for repurposing. Of course, check a book's worth before crafting or making art with it (SEE PAGE 23).

GIFTING BOOKS

Gifting books is another way to preserve them. By allowing a book to live on in another person's library, you prolong its readability and collectability. As mentioned in chapter 2, I believe books are the only acceptable re-gift item because you are not simply giving a physical object but an experience, that of the book's content. Books are incredibly intimate gifts because you are sharing ideas with another person, proclaiming what you identify with and what you think is good, true, and relevant. It shifts the private experience of reading to a public one, and in this way, you are giving a piece of yourself.

Before giving a book as a gift, consider personalizing it with an inscription. Writing a simple *to* and *from* and the date is sufficient, but adding a message relating to the context of the exchange makes it even more special.

Another form of gifting books is donating in memoriam to a library. Granting a single book, a limited collection, or an entire library in memory of someone who has passed continues that person's legacy, as well as the legacy of the books themselves. Whether you are donating to a public library, school library, or a personal library, a simple bookplate on the front page printed with *Donated in memory of . . .* is a thoughtful way to remember someone and memorialize the topics about which he or she was passionate.

Many years ago I experienced firsthand the power of an "in memoriam" bookplate and have never forgotten its impact on me. While teaching at an art college, I met a student named Harvey, a retired newspaper editor in his sixties, who was finally back in school to follow his passion for painting and drawing. An ideal student, he was totally committed to his studies, yet had a notoriously tough outer shell. I was much younger than him at the time, and he tested my adeptness and knowledge. By mid-semester, I'd passed his trials and was in his good graces, and we became friends. He would bring me books from the library, new art titles that had just come in that he thought I'd like, and I was always profoundly touched.

Years later, when I was no longer teaching at that school, I ran into an old colleague who told me Harvey had recently passed away. I was saddened by this news, especially since he had not completed his degree, which had been so important to him. A few weeks later I borrowed some art books from the city library, one of which was a Robert Rauschenberg monograph. I got back to the studio, sat down, and opened the book. Inside was a bookplate that read, *Donated in Memoriam from the Library of Harvey L.* It was as if Harvey had brought me that book himself, just as he used to do.

CONSERVING

Book conservation is the art of repairing books. Whether you caused the damage or found it that way, if you know how to repair general problems and minor infractions, you can better tend to what you own and acquire. Following are instructions for how to mend general wear and tear, as well as instructions for making a slipcase to protect an especially delicate volume.

THE CONSERVATOR'S TOOLBOX

Before beginning any book conservation project, gather the tools and materials shown here. You might also want to familiarize yourself with the anatomy of a book and some basic techniques used for repairs (SEE RIGHT).

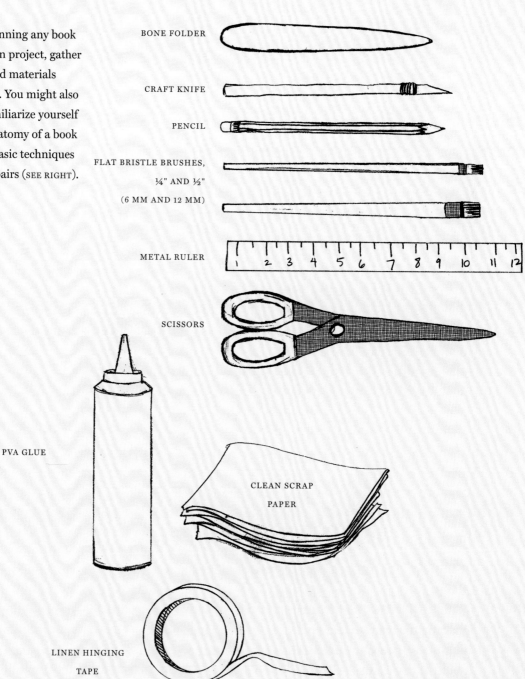

BONE FOLDER

CRAFT KNIFE

PENCIL

FLAT BRISTLE BRUSHES,
¼" AND ½"
(6 MM AND 12 MM)

METAL RULER

SCISSORS

PVA GLUE

CLEAN SCRAP
PAPER

LINEN HINGING
TAPE

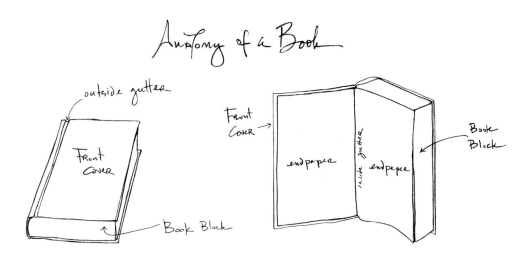

Anatomy of a Book

outside gutter

Front Cover

Front Cover

Book Block

Front Cover

endpaper

inside gutter

endpaper

Book Block

Book Block

BASIC TECHNIQUES USED IN REPAIR

Gluing

The industry standard glue to use is called PVA (polyvinyl acetate), an archival glue that will not yellow or crack over time. When instructions call for gluing, always use glue sparingly, applying it from the center out to the edges, being sure to cover the entire surface evenly. Excess glue will ooze out and/or create ripples when drying. Always work on a clean surface and use clean scrap paper when gluing.

Checking Paper Grain

All papers have an invisible, though very significant, element called the grain. Paper is made from fibers, and the grain is the direction in which those fibers are set when the paper is made. Pages and the boards that make up the book covers also have a grain, since they, too, are made from paper. When adding new paper to your books, it is important that all the grains are going in the same direction; otherwise things will warp. To find the grain of your paper, simply hold the ends and bow it toward you. If you feel resistance, that is not the grain side. The grain side will bow easily and softly. You will also find the paper tears and folds more easily along the grain. The grain of a book cover is most often parallel to the spine.

Employing Kozo Paper

Kozo is a durable Japanese tissue paper made from vegetable fibers. It is used in book conservation because it is archival, strong, and thin. It is tear-resistant and flexible, making it ideal for hinging. It is also referred to as Japanese mending paper or hinging tissue, and is available at artist supply and bookbinding stores.

Replacing Endpapers

Endpapers keep the book block inside of its covers and act as the inner hinge. They are often colored or patterned, and are always heavier in weight than the text page. It is not uncommon for endpapers to wear and tear with time, so that the book itself comes loose from its covers. You might want to replace damaged endpapers or even give undamaged ones a new design (which can be a nice touch if the book is a gift). Whether you are repairing or redesigning, the process is the same. If there are any significant bookplates or meaningful inscriptions on the original endpapers, be sure to remove and reattach them to the new endpapers.

MATERIALS

Replacement paper in a weight similar to the original endpapers (SEE NOTE)

Kozo paper

Waxed paper

TOOLS

Conservator's Toolbox (SEE PAGE 78)

Sandpaper (OPTIONAL)

NOTE: *If the replacement paper is too thin, it will not be able to support the weight of the book block and will tear easily. A heavyweight paper is good, as are any artist papers. It is best to use an archival paper, especially if the book is historically valuable.*

BEFORE *Worn endpapers have torn completely, freeing the book from its covers.*

AFTER *New endpapers ensure a book's longevity.*

I   GENTLY PULL OR CUT OUT
OLD ENDPAPERS

1 If the endpapers are already quite loose, you might be able to gently pull them free. Otherwise, remove the endpapers from both the front and back of the book with a craft knife, carefully slicing along the inside gutter. This will free the book block from its cover. Discard the endpaper attached to the book block. If the endpapers glued to the inside covers are peeling, remove any loose pieces. Depending on the condition, you might also lightly sand the inside covers for a smoother surface.

2 Size and cut replacement paper, making sure the grain of the paper (see page 79) is parallel to the grain of the spine, to prevent warping. Measure the height and width of the endpaper that is still attached to the inside cover and double its width. Cut two pieces of paper to these dimensions. Fold each piece in half, with the patterned or colored sides facing inward.

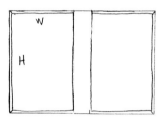

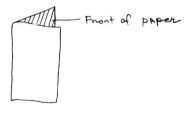

Front of paper

2   size, cut, and fold replacement endpapers

3 Cut two strips of Kozo paper to the following dimensions: ½" (12 mm) wide × the height of the endpaper + 1" (2.5 cm). Fold each strip in half lengthwise, then open. Place a piece of waxed paper on your work surface and set the folded Kozo paper on top. Using the crease mark as a guide, cover half the width of the Kozo strip with a piece of scrap paper, leaving ¼" (6 mm) exposed. Use a ¼" (6 mm) bristle brush to apply glue along that edge. Discard the scrap paper and align the crease edge of the new endpaper along this edge. Be aware of top and bottom if your endpaper has a directional pattern. Smooth with a bone folder. Do the same with the second new endpaper. Weight all and allow to dry for about 15 minutes, then trim any excess Kozo paper from the top or bottom edge.

4 Apply glue to the other half of the tissue. Place the endpaper with the Kozo strip precisely on top of the book block, squaring it up at the corners and with its hinge edge aligned with the book block's spine. The tissue will hang over the spine to attach. Smooth out and press with a bone folder for full adhesion. Repeat on the second endpaper. Allow 15 minutes for drying.

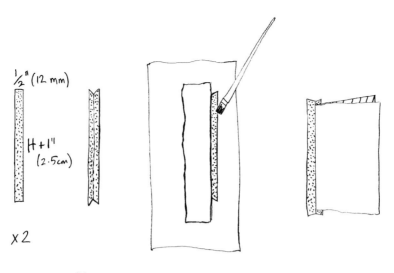

½" (12 mm)

H+1"
(2.5cm)

x2

3   CUT AND GLUE KOZO PAPER TO NEW ENDPAPERS

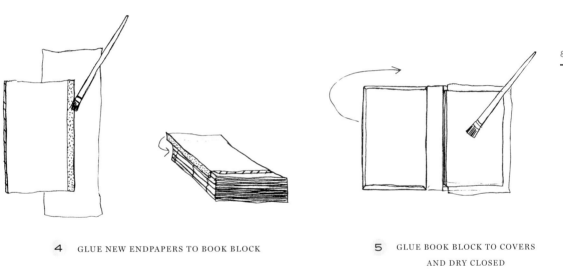

4   GLUE NEW ENDPAPERS TO BOOK BLOCK

5   GLUE BOOK BLOCK TO COVERS
AND DRY CLOSED

5 Open the book's cover, laying it flat, and place the book block on the inside back cover, aligning and squaring up the edges. Gently open the new front endpaper and place a piece of waxed paper beneath. Apply glue, brushing from the center out to the edges of the paper, then close the cover and press. Open it and smooth the adhesion to the inside cover with the bone folder and close again. Flip the book over to the back and repeat. When complete, weight the book and allow it to dry overnight.

Replacing Covers

The role of book covers is to encase and protect the book's pages. When a book's covers are terribly worn, warped, stained, or otherwise unsightly, you'll want to make new covers (also called recasing). This is also a good technique to create custom covers for a gift or if you want to recase a book that has a less-than-appealing cover. And it can be used to convert a paperback into a hardcover.

MATERIALS

⅛" (3 mm) book board
    (also called chipboard)

Ribbon (optional)

Kozo paper

Waxed paper

Paper or bookcloth for covers

Bookcloth or leather for spine

TOOLS

Conservator's Toolbox
(SEE PAGE 78)

BEFORE *The linen of this cover has torn in several places and compromises the life of the pages within.*

AFTER *A portion of the original spine is placed on the new one and a ribbon page marker is added.*

| CUT BOOK BLOCK FROM COVERS

1 Remove the book block completely from its covers. You might need to cut through the inside gutter of the endpapers with a craft knife to remove it fully. If there is any important information on the spine or the endpapers, save it for reapplication. (For instance, if the spine displays the title or some nice decorative pattern, you can re-glue it to the new spine.)

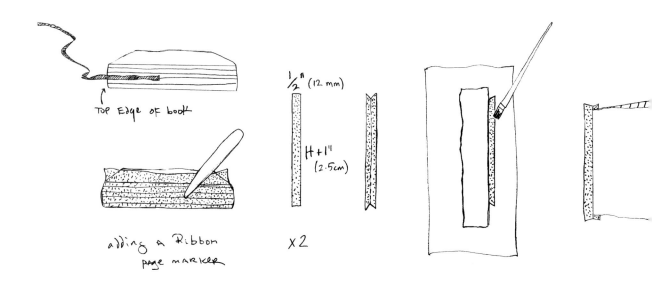

TOP EDGE OF BOOK

½" (12 mm)

H+1" (2.5cm)

adding a Ribbon page marker

x2

2 If you choose to add a ribbon page marker, cut a length of ribbon that measures the height of the book plus 4" (10 cm) and tack it to the book block's spine with a spot of glue.

If the spine of the book block is loose, reinforce it by cutting a piece of Kozo paper to cover the height and width of the spine, adding 1" (2.5 cm) to its width. Place the cut paper on a piece of waxed paper and brush glue on. Align it onto the book block's spine and press it into the grooves of the signatures with the bone folder. Set aside to dry. When you have completed the entire process of re-covering the book, trim any excess ribbon at the end, cutting it at a 45-degree angle.

3 Attach new endpapers (SEE PAGE 80).

4 Cut the book boards: Be sure the grain of the book board is parallel to the spine (SEE PAGE 79).

MAKE THE COVERS: Measure the height and width of the book block, adding ⅛" (3 mm) to the width and ¼" (6 mm) to the height for overhang. Mark and cut two pieces with these dimensions.

MAKE THE SPINE: Measure the depth and height of the spine. (The height of the spine is the same measurement as the height of your covers.) Mark and cut one piece with these dimensions.

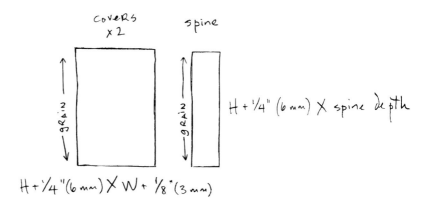

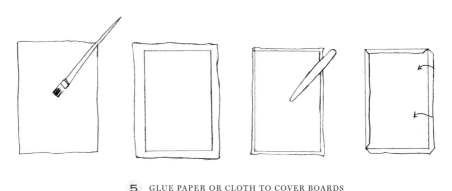

COVERS
x 2

spine

grain

grain

H + ¼" (6 mm) X spine depth

H + ¼" (6 mm) X W + ⅛" (3 mm)

4 MEASURE AND CUT BOOK BOARDS
FOR COVER AND SPINE

5 GLUE PAPER OR CLOTH TO COVER BOARDS

5 Cover the boards with either paper or bookcloth. If using paper to cover the boards, be sure its grain is parallel to the grain of the cover boards. Cut two pieces of paper or cloth to the size of the boards, adding ½" (12 mm) to the measurements on all sides. Place the paper or cloth facedown on scrap paper and brush glue on the back side, then place the board on top, centering it. Flip the covered board over onto a clean surface. Push out any air pockets by gently smoothing the paper or cloth from the center out with the long side of the bone folder.

Flip the covered board back over, and trim the paper at the corners, leaving about ⅛" (3 mm) of paper. Lift the paper over the edge and onto the back of the cover with the bone folder, pressing the paper to adhere. Press the paper in at the corners to cover any exposed board. You might need to brush a little more glue on some places.

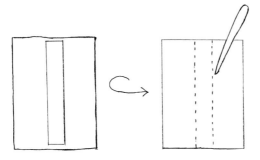

6   GLUE CLOTH OR LEATHER TO SPINE BOARD.
SCORE HINGES WITH BONE FOLDER

88

6 Make the spine materials: It is best to use cloth or leather for the spine since it is more flexible and will withstand the hinging action of opening and closing the book over time. Cut the material of choice to fit the spine board to the following dimensions: spine height + 1" (2.5 cm) × spine width + 4" (10 cm).

Place the material right side down on a piece of scrap paper and brush glue on the back side, mostly in the area where the spine will go. Place the spine board on top, centering it. Flip it over and smooth with the bone folder. Run the bone folder along each side of the spine's length to start creating the hinge.

7 Assemble the covers: Place the spine construction right side down on a clean piece of scrap paper. Gauge the hinge distance: A distance of ¼" (6 mm) between the spine and the cover is typical, but a thicker or larger book might need a little more space. Measure your hinge distance from each edge of the spine, and mark this line with a pencil and ruler.

Brush glue on the entire exposed area of the spine material. Then, with right sides down, place the front and back covers onto the spine material, aligning the inner edge of each cover along the hinge line. Be sure the top edges of all three pieces are aligned so they are straight

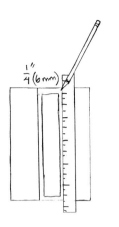

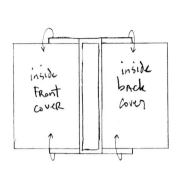

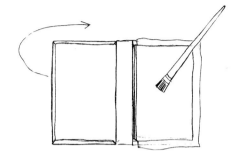

7   MARK HINGE PLACEMENT AND
GLUE COVERS TO SPINE

8   GLUE COVERS TO BOOK BLOCK
AND DRY CLOSED

and even. (And make sure your covers are not upside down!)

Carefully flip the new cover over and smooth out any air pockets with the bone folder. Press the material into the gutters with the point of the bone folder to further score the hinge. Flip the book back over. Fold the margin of the spine material over to wrap onto the back side of the covers and press into place with the tip of the bone folder.

8 Re-encase the book block: With the new covers open, place the book block on the inside back cover, fitting it into place while aligning the spine of the book block at the inner edge of the back cover. Close the front cover and be sure the book block is in straight.

Open the front cover. Place a clean piece of scrap paper between the new endpapers and brush glue on the back side facing you. Pull the scrap out and close the cover, pressing down to adhere. Open the cover and smooth out the endpaper with the bone folder.

Flip the book over and do the same on the back. Weight the book and allow to set overnight.

Making a Slipcase

When you have a book that is very delicate from age, a slipcase is a great protective shell that leaves the book's spine visible. It is also good for grouping together books in a series, especially thin paperbacks.

MATERIALS

⅛" (3 mm) book board (also called chipboard)

½ yard (.5 m) ribbon (¼" or ½" [6 mm or 12 mm] width)

Decorative paper or bookcloth

TOOLS

Conservator's Toolbox
(SEE PAGE 78)

1 Measure the height, width, and depth of the book to be slipcased and add ⅛" (3 mm) on all sides. You want the book to fit snugly into the finished case yet easily slip in and out. Mark the measurements onto the book board as shown in the diagram on page 92. You'll be drawing five panels: front, back, top, bottom, and depth.

Once you have drawn these lines, cut out the entire form with a craft knife. Then score the four inside edges by running the craft knife only halfway through the board's thickness.

2 Flip the board over and glue 4" (10 cm) of the ribbon to the center of the inside back panel as shown in illustration 2 on the next page. This will help release the book from the case once it is assembled.

top

SCORE

front   SCORE depth SCORE   back

inside

4" (10 cm)

SCORE

bottom

| MEASURE AND CUT SLIPCASE FORM FROM BOOK BOARD

2   GLUE RIBBON TO INSIDE BACK PANEL

3 Fold the score lines to create the box shape, applying linen tape to the outside edges of the box to hold it together and to reinforce the joints.

4 Measure the width and total length of the slipcase's depth and add 1" (2.5 cm). Then measure the height and width of the front and back panels and add ½" (12 mm) to the width only. Cut the paper or bookcloth to these dimensions, being sure the grain of the paper is parallel to the grain of the box's boards.

Lay the long sheet of paper facedown on a piece of scrap paper and brush glue on the back side. With the case standing upright, center the paper strip along the top edge, allowing a ½" (12 mm) overhang at the opening. Press into place and wrap over the corner along the depth edge. Use the bone folder throughout to get the edges smooth and crisp. Turn the case one rotation and wrap the paper onto the bottom edge, using the same technique.

Trim the paper at the corners and fold it over along the front and back panels, tucking the overhang into the inside of the slipcase.

Apply the paper to the front and back in a similar way: gluing, aligning the corners, smoothing out with the bone folder, and tucking the overhang into the case's interior.

Notch the paper at the point of the ribbon. Allow to dry overnight.

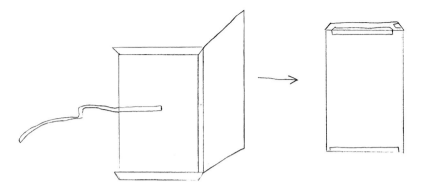

3   FOLD SCORE LINES AND TAPE BOX JOINTS

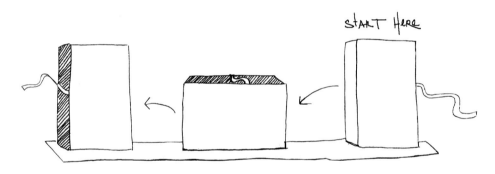

START HERE

4   APPLY GLUE TO PAPER STRIP AND PRESS BOX INTO PLACE.
ROTATE TO COVER ALL SIDES

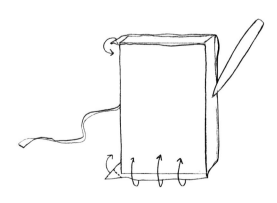

5   GLUE PAPER TO BOX FRONT AND BACK

PRESERVING AND CONSERVING

Tipping in a Page

When a page has fallen out or loosened from its binding, you can glue it back into place, a procedure known as "tipping in." Tipping in is used to reattach a single page. If too many pages are loose (say, more than three), it is better to rebind the entire book. (This might be a job for a conservator; to tackle it yourself, you might want to get some guides on rebinding.)

TOOLS

Conservator's Toolbox
(SEE PAGE 78)

1 Open the book to where the page is missing. Some books (usually those with sewn bindings) will lay flat, while other books (usually those with glued bindings) will need to be propped open. If you need to prop the book open, simply place a pencil inside. To avoid putting strain on the spine, support it by setting a stack of books against one outside board.

Begin by tucking the detached page back into its proper place to see exactly how it will fit. You want it to sit snugly into the gutter of the book, so that it does not hang past the book block on any edge; it should be flush with all the edges.

2 Lay the detached page on a work surface with the backside facing up. Place a sheet of scrap paper over the loose page, leaving about ⅛" (3 mm) of the loose sheet's interior edge exposed. Using a small bristle brush, apply glue along that edge. Discard the scrap paper and place the glued page into the book as you practiced in step 1.

3 Place a fresh sheet of scrap paper over the reinserted page and run a bone folder along its inner edge at the gutter to smooth it into place. Close the book, weight it, and allow it to set overnight.

1   PROP BOOK OPEN TO MISSING PAGE

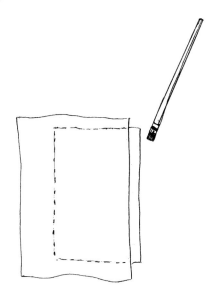

2   APPLY GLUE TO PAGE EDGE

3   REINSERT PAGE AND SMOOTH IN PLACE

PRESERVING AND CONSERVING

CHAPTER FOUR

CRAFTING WITH BOOKS

LIKE GIFTING BOOKS, CRAFTING WITH BOOKS MAKES THE INTIMATE ACT OF COLLECTING, READING, AND OWNING BOOKS A PUBLIC ONE. CREATING VISUAL FORMS WITH BOOKS NOT ONLY ADDS A LITERARY AND THOUGHTFUL SLANT TO AN INTERIOR SPACE, BUT UNVEILS YOUR INNER BIBLIOPHILE. THIS CHAPTER CONSISTS OF TWO SECTIONS, REPURPOSED PROJECTS AND DIGITAL PROJECTS.

REPURPOSED PROJECTS

You may have an accumulation of some books that are simply too damaged, obsolete (think: old textbooks) or lacking in value (sorry, Jackie Collins!) to maintain in your collection or donate. These are the perfect books to use as materials for creating objects from books. The repurposed projects are designed to transform these tired volumes. This is a bit of an extension of my previous book, *The Repurposed Library*, a book solely dedicated to repurposing old books into new forms. By crafting forms with actual books we are drawing our attention to their physical details, such as the visual texture of printed text and the poetry of worn covers, all the while honoring their inherent appeal.

DIGITAL PROJECTS

There might be some titles in your library that you adore beyond words, and how nice would it be to let them have a larger presence in your everyday settings? These are the books you would never deconstruct, for their value—whether strictly sentimental or fully financial—is too high. The digital projects are designed to employ scanning and printing files in order to create visual forms, rather than using the actual book, allowing you to preserve your collections while still crafting with them. And because you are digitizing them you do not need to necessarily own or buy the books you use; you can borrow them from your local library or from friends. All you need is a personal computer with photoediting software, such as Photoshop, a scanner, and a printer. When choosing material to scan or print, keep in mind copyright law. If you are reproducing printed material for single and private use only you do not need to be concerned with copyright law. However, if you plan on sharing or selling objects made with printed material, you must abide the copyright law. As a general rule, copyright infringement is when a copyrighted work is reproduced, distributed, publicly displayed, or made into a derivative work without the permission of the copyright owner. For more information visit copyright.gov.

Page Pouf

Purely decorative yet highly legible, these plush spheres are simple and very inexpensive to make. Consider the color and tone of the book pages that you use for the look you want, as well as their condition: Pages that are brittle will crease and crumble. Two different sizes are shown here.

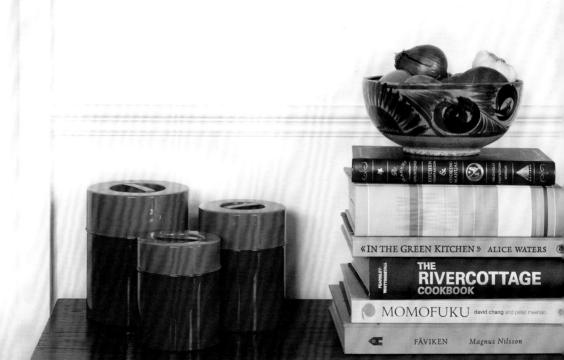

«IN THE GREEN KITCHEN» ALICE WATERS

THE
RIVERCOTTAGE
COOKBOOK

MOMOFUKU david chang and peter meehan

FÄVIKEN   Magnus Nilsson

5" (12 cm) Styrofoam ball
(and/or 4" [10 cm] Styrofoam ball)

120 book pages (counting each front and back
as one) cut to 4" (10 cm) squares
(for a 4" [10 cm] sphere: 100 book pages cut to
3" [7.5 cm] squares)

Wooden dowel, ½" (12 mm) diameter × 3"
(7.5 cm) long (a standard tube of lip balm
works, too)

36" (1 m) length of filament per sphere

One ball-headed pin per sphere

Cup hook, for hanging

Hot glue gun and glue sticks

1 Attach the hanging cord: At the base of the pin's head, tie the filament on with a knot and insert the pin into the Styrofoam ball. Put a drop of hot glue at its base to secure it. This will be the top of your form.

2 Create a tufted page: Place the flat end of the dowel (or one end of your lip balm tube) in the center of one of the page squares. Lift the page up around the dowel, allowing it to ruffle and slightly fold while keeping the bottom flat. With the dowel still inside the tuft, put a drop of hot glue on the flat bottom and place it on the sphere, beginning at the top beside the pinhead. Press and hold in place for 10 seconds to set the glue, then remove the dowel. Repeat this process, snugly placing each tuft beside the others so that none of the Styrofoam shows.

3 As the form becomes more and more filled, brace the sphere with the tips of your fingers between the tufts to avoid crushing them. Once the form is completely covered, hang it from a cup hook screwed into the ceiling.

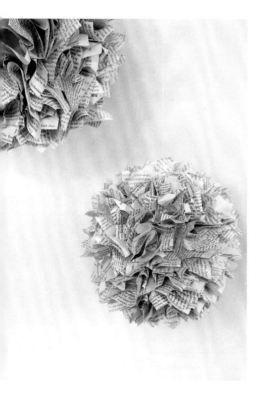

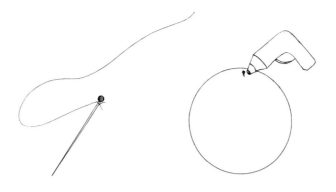

1   TIE HANGING CORD TO PIN AND GLUE
TO STYROFOAM FORM

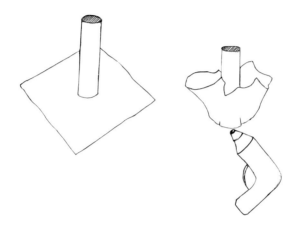

2   WRAP PAGE AROUND DOWEL AND GLUE
TO STYROFOAM FORM

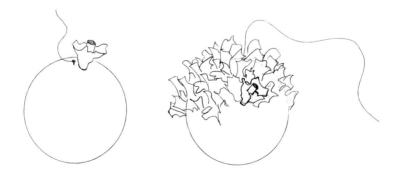

3   GLUE REMAINING TUFTS TO STYROFOAM FORM

Literary Profiles

Text makes compelling visual texture when creating graphic art, and these silhouettes cut from book pages are no exception. Inexpensive and easy to make, they are highly individual on their own, but can be further customized by your choice of book page. Consider using the sitter's favorite book for a portrait in profile. Also consider illustrated books and atlases. Here I used pages from a cookbook, an antique math primer, *Alice in Wonderland*, and an antiquated map to further personalize my profiles.

Book page (SEE NOTE)

Photograph of a person in profile

Craft knife

Cutting mat

Tracing paper

5 × 7" (12 × 17 cm) piece of mat board
(any color of your choice)

5 × 7" (12 × 17 cm) frame with glass

NOTE: *If you want to use a page from a book that you
do not want to deconstruct, simply scan it and print it, or
make a color photocopy.*

Computer and printer

Fine-point Sharpie marker

Light box (optional)

Masking tape

Pencil and eraser

Glue and flat brush

1 With photo editing software (like Photoshop) or a photocopier, size your photo to fit nicely within a 5 × 7" (12 × 17 cm) space, making it no wider than 4" (10 cm). Print it out.

2 Trace the silhouette: Lay tracing paper on top of the photo and trace the outline with a Sharpie, getting as much detail in the outline as possible.

Place the silhouette down on a light box and secure it with a couple of pieces of tape. Place the book page on top of the tracing paper and secure it with tape. Turn on the light box and trace the silhouette onto the book page with a pencil. (If you do not have a light box, simply tape the silhouette to a sunny window, tape the book page on top of it, and trace.)

3 Cut out the profile. Working on a cutting mat, run the craft knife along your drawn lines on the book page. Go slowly and use short strokes for accuracy. Once fully cut, erase any bit of remaining pencil line.

4 Mount the profile onto mat board. Brush a sparing amount of glue on the back side of the profile and place it on the piece of mat board. Allow to dry for 10 minutes and then insert the mat and glass into the frame.

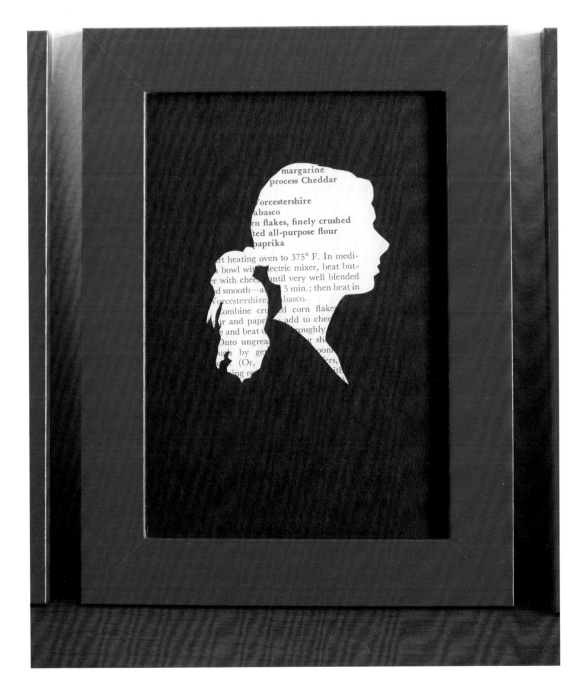

Pocket Notecards

The gratification of getting a handwritten note in the mailbox over the ding of an e-mail in your inbox makes these library-inspired notecards delectable. Make a set for yourself to send or give a set as a gift. Cards and envelopes are often sold in groups of ten, so you might want to create a set of ten, or two sets of five. The envelopes are lined with book pages, so consider the types of pages you want to use (for example, illustrated or text only) when you are choosing your stationery colors.

Ten sheets 8½ × 11" (A4) paper
(your choice of color)

Ten 4⅜" × 5¾" (A2) envelopes
(your choice of color)

Book pockets

Book borrower cards

Cardboard (non-corrugated),
5½ × 8" (14 × 20 cm)

Book pages measuring no less than
5 × 8" (12 × 20 cm)

Computer and printer, or rubber stamp
and ink pad

Glue stick

Craft knife

Cutting mat

Pencil

Metal ruler

110

1 Create the cards: With your computer printer or a rubber stamp, print these phrases onto the lower righthand corner of the 8½ × 11" (A4) paper, as follows:

ON 5 SHEETS: *check this out. . .*
ON 5 SHEETS: *a long overdue hello*

Fold the paper in half widthwise and then in half lengthwise, making a folded card with the printed phrase on the front.
Using the glue stick, glue the book pocket to the inside of each card. Slip a book borrower card inside the pocket. This is where you will write your note.

2 Make the envelope liner template: Open the flap of the envelope and lay it flat on top of the cardboard, aligning the bottom edges to get it straight, then slide the envelope down about ½" (12 mm). Trace the flap and envelope side and remove the envelope. Cut out the envelope liner template.

3 Line the envelopes with book pages: Place the template on top of the book page, being sure to center it. Trace the liner shape onto the book page and cut it out. Slip the page liner into the envelope. Fold and crease the flap of the liner along the envelope's inside flap crease. Run glue on the back of the liner flap and press the envelope flap down on it to secure.

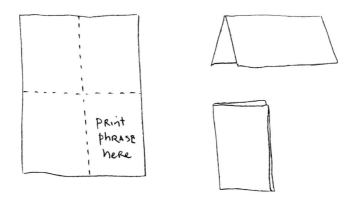

1   FOLD PAPER INTQ FOURTHS TO CREATE
FOLDED CARDS

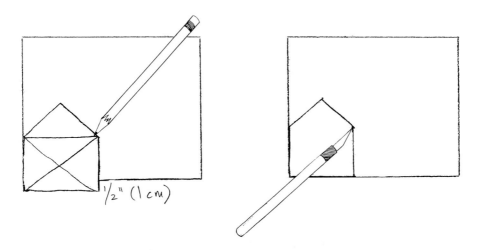

1/2" (1 cm)

2   TRACE AND CUT ENVELOPE LINER TEMPLATE

3   CUT PAGES TO TEMPLATE AND PLACE INSIDE ENVELOPE.
GLUE LINER TO ENVELOPE FLAP TO SECURE

Book Cover Bunting

This simple vertical bunting becomes a modern textile when hung on the wall or freely suspended. Consider making several and creating a backdrop. This is a great use of old, worn covers or, if you've made the Bedside Reading Headboard (page 116), the ones remaining from that project. Group together five front and back book covers according to color and/or theme.

MATERIALS

Book covers, 5 pairs (back and front)

3 yards (3 m), 1" (2.5 cm) twill tape

TOOLS

Craft knife

Pencil

Metal ruler

Scissors

Hot glue gun and glue sticks

1 Prep each of the book covers: Begin by removing the book block completely from its covers by carefully cutting with the craft knife through the inside gutter of the endpapers (SEE PAGE 80). Set the book block aside for another use. Then cut along the outside gutter of the covers to free the back and front covers from the spine. Discard the spines or use them for another purpose.

Lay the five pairs of book covers in a vertical line with about 2" (5 cm) between each. Measure the length from the top of the topmost book cover pairing to the middle of the bottom book cover pairing. Add 12" (30.5 cm) to this and cut the twill tape to this length.

2 Assemble the bunting: Lift the front cover off of each cover pair and, with a pencil and ruler, mark the center width at the top edge of the inside back book cover. This is to guide where you will place the twill tape.

3 Starting at the topmost book cover and leaving 12" (30.5 cm) of extra twill tape extending above the cover, run a line of hot glue in the center of the inside back cover and center the twill tape along it using your mark as a guide.

Run hot glue all over the back side of the front cover and place the front cover over the back cover, sandwiching the twill tape between them.

Continue until all five covers are glued together, encasing the twill tape. Then make a loop in the twill at the top to hang the bunting.

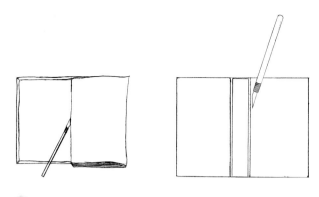

1 PREP BOOK COVERS BY REMOVING BOOK BLOCKS AND SPINES

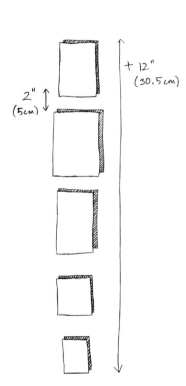

+ 12"
(30.5 cm)

2"
(5 cm)

2 LAY OUT COVERS. MEASURE AND
   CUT TWILL TAPE

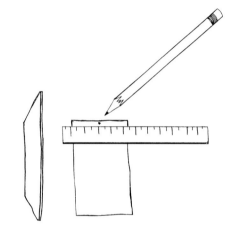

3 MARK TOP CENTER OF EACH INSIDE BACK COVER
   TO GUIDE PLACEMENT OF TWILL TAPE

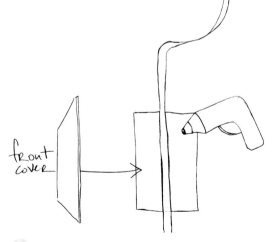

front
cover

4 GLUE FRONT COVER TO BACK COVER,
   SANDWICHING TWILL TAPE BETWEEN

Bedside Reading Headboard

Books add intimacy to a bedroom, and this headboard is designed to do just that. Discarded book spines are aligned in bands of organized color and punctuated by a circle of text, for a modernizing punch of geometry. I used pages from Freud's *Interpretation of Dreams* for the circle. This simple piece is created like a puzzle, with various book spines abutting and interlocking seamlessly. The finished piece hangs flush on the wall, about 12" (30.5 cm) from the top of the mattress. Customize the colors and/ or subject matter according to those slumbering below.

Approximately 85 hardcover books, depending upon their size

½" (12 mm) plywood board cut to 18 × 60" (46 × 152 cm) (to fit a queen-size bed)

Approximately 14 loose book pages, depending upon their size

22 × 30" (55 × 76 cm) sheet poster board

3 mounting screws with wall anchors

Drill and ¼" (6 mm) drill bit

Metal ruler

Craft knife

Pencil

Scissors

White glue and glue brush

Bone folder

Acrylic varnish or Mod Podge

1" (2.5 cm) sponge brush

Hot glue gun and glue sticks

Spray varnish

118
—

BELOW *Book spines, freed from their covers, are tiled into a mosaic of color and text.*

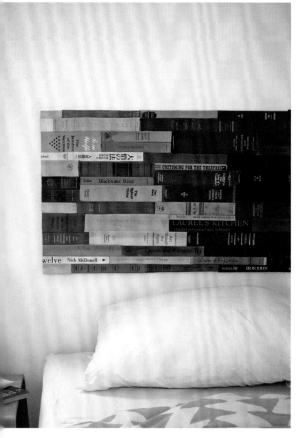

1 On the back of the plywood board, drill three equidistant holes for hanging, 6" (15 cm) down from the top edge, one in the center of the board and the other two flanking it, 15" (38 cm) in from each side.

2 For each book, remove the book block completely from its covers by carefully cutting through the inside gutter of the endpapers with a craft knife. (Reserve the book block for another project, such as the Page Pouf on page 100, Literary Profiles on page 104, or Pocket Note Cards on page 108.) Cut the spine along the outermost edge of the outside gutter to free it from the covers. You want this little bit of extra gutter fabric to then fold under to make a clean, finished edge when you glue the spines to the board.

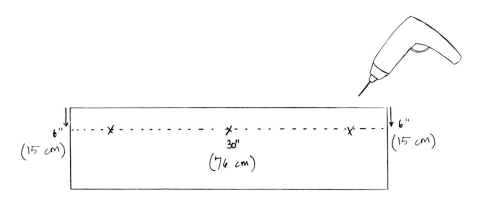

1 DRILL THREE EQUIDISTANT HOLES ON
   BACK OF PLYWOOD FOR HANGING

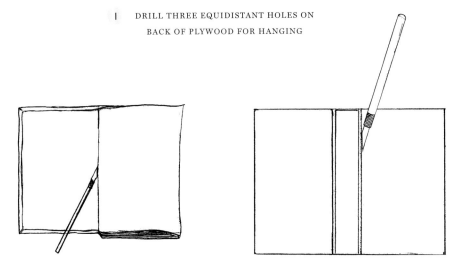

2 REMOVE BOOK BLOCK AND SPINE.
   FOLD GUTTER FABRIC UNDER

3 Make the circle template: Cut a 20" (50 cm) circle from the poster board (either trace something with that diameter or tie a 24" (60 cm) length of string to a pencil, tape it to the center of the poster board, and draw out the circle using the pencil and string as a makeshift compass). Cut out the circle with scissors.

4 Create the circle of pages: Position the circle template on the plywood board and trace around it with a pencil; set the template aside. Working page by page, brush white glue on the back of each book page and align them in rows within the traced circle, using the bone folder to smooth out any air pockets; the pages will overlap the circle's edge.

Once all the pages are glued down, realign and re-trace the circle template over the book pages, then brush a coat of varnish over them. Allow to fully dry.

5 Attach the spines to the board: Spend a little time laying out the design of the headboard and deciding which spines to place where. Consider their size and their color.

When you have a pleasing design, begin attaching the spines that will fall around the edge of the circle. Holding a spine in place along the edge of the circle, fit the circle template on top of it and trace the arc of that portion of the circle onto the spine. Cut along this line with scissors and, being sure the spine edges are folded under, hot-glue the spine down. Repeat with the remaining spines that will fall along the circle to outline the circle.

Then continue hot-gluing spines out to the headboard's edges, fitting each spine next to those you have already adhered before gluing it down. When complete, spray the headboard with spray varnish.

6 Install the headboard: Measure and mark where the headboard will go (about 12" [30.5 cm] from the top of the mattress and centered over the bed). Install three screws with wall anchors, positioning them to align with the holes you drilled into the back of the headboard—one screw above the center of the bed and two screws flanking it, 15" (38 cm) from the center screw on either side. Leave the screws extending out from the wall by about ³⁄₈" (1 cm). Fit the screw heads into the holes in the back of the headboard to allow the headboard to lie flush to the wall.

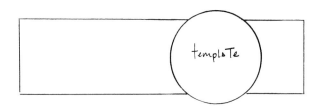

3   CUT CIRCLE TEMPLATE FROM POSTER BOARD

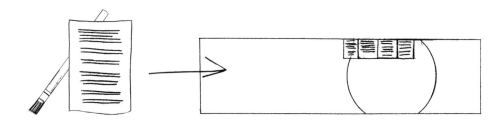

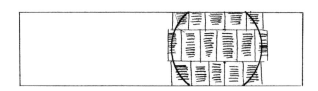

4   TRACE TEMPLATE ONTO PLYWOOD BOARD
     AND GLUE ON BOOK PAGES

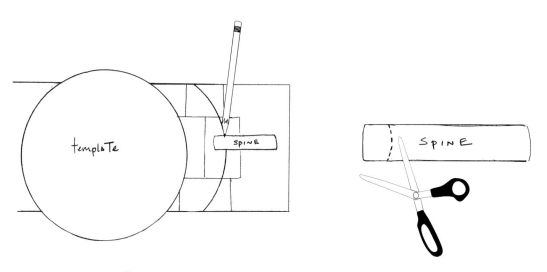

5   GLUE SPINES TO BOARD. TRIM SPINES THAT FALL ALONG CIRCLE

Storytime Mobile

Miniature books are highly collectible mostly because of their diminutive scale, which must technically measure around $2 \times 1\frac{1}{2}"$ (5×4 cm) to qualify a book as such. For this mobile I made my own facsimile versions of miniatures by scanning book covers and title pages from vintage children's books and resizing them. In miniature form, these books become tiny artworks as they hang suspended from above, silently spinning their stories.

⅜" (1 cm) thick, 24" (60 cm) long basswood strip
   cut in half, or two 12" (30.5 cm) long strips

12 × 12" (30.5 × 30.5 cm) piece of ¼" (6 mm)
   foam core

Monofilament (fishing line)

Four books

Eyelet screw or cotter pin, ½" (12 mm) long
   (I used a ¾" [2 cm] brass cotter pin)

Four sheets drawing paper, cut to 8½ × 11"
   (A4 size)

Clear varnish

1" (2.5 cm) foam brush

Sandpaper

Pencil and metal ruler

Power drill and ⁵⁄₆₄" (2 mm) drill bit

Hot glue gun and glue sticks

Computer, scanner, and printer

Craft knife

Scissors

Craft glue and glue brush

Bone folder

Sewing needle

1 Make the armature: Apply two coats of varnish to the basswood strips, sanding them between coats as needed. Once the varnish is completely dry, measure and mark 2" (5 cm) in from each end of both pieces of basswood and drill a hole through the wood. Next, mark the center of each strip and drill a hole there.

   Cross the two pieces of basswood to form 90° angles (making a plus sign) and hot-glue them together at the center.

2 Create the book images: Scan in the covers and title pages of each of the four books. Using photoediting software (like Photoshop), size each image proportionately with a width of 3" (7.5 cm); the lengths will vary slightly. Pair each cover and title page on a single layout with at least ¾" (2 cm) between them and print each pairing out onto a sheet of the drawing paper. (Or color-photocopy the cover and title pages together to print on one page, reducing the percentage to make each 3" [7.5 cm] wide.)

   Cut the cover image from the paper, adding a ¾" (2 cm) margin of extra paper on all sides. Cut out the corresponding title page at its exact edges.

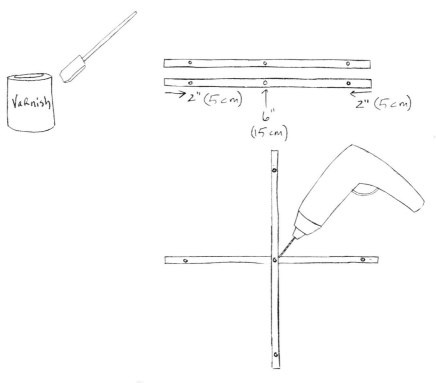

1   VARNISH BASSWOOD STRIPS. MARK AND DRILL HOLES INTO
STRIPS AND GLUE AT CENTER TO CREATE ARMATURE

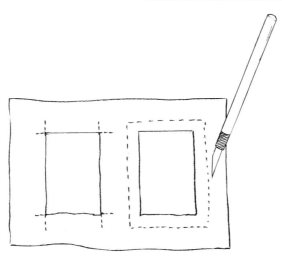

2   SCAN AND CUT BOOK IMAGES

3 Make the miniature hanging books: Measure the exact size of each title page image (excluding the ¾" [2 cm] border) and cut one piece of foam core per book to fit. Brush glue on the back of the cover image and place the foam core on it, centering it exactly. Use the bone folder to smooth out the front of the image. Trim the corners, apply glue to the edges, and wrap the edges around to the back of the foam core. Use the bone folder to smooth the edges against the foam core.

Brush glue on the back of the title page image and adhere it to the back side of the foam core, positioning it to cover the folded edges of the front cover and using the bone folder to smooth the paper.

4 Assemble the mobile: Insert the eyelet screw through the hole drilled at the center of the armature. Attach an 18" (46 cm) length of monofilament, tying it through the loop of the eyelet and then making a knotted loop at the end that will hang from the ceiling.

With a pencil and ruler, measure and mark the top center of each miniature book, about ⅛" (3 mm) in from the edge.

Cut four 18" (46 cm) lengths of monofilament. Thread a needle with one length of monofilament and insert it through the foam core at the center mark. Knot the filament and then draw it through one of the drilled holes in the armature; knot to secure. Repeat with the remaining three books. Adjust and vary the lengths of monofilament as you see fit.

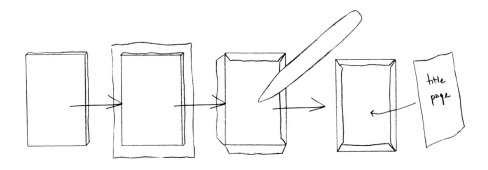

3   GLUE COVER IMAGES TO FOAM CORE

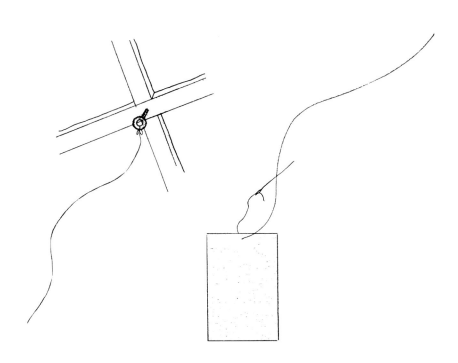

4   ATTACH FILAMENTS TO EYELET SCREW AND
TOP CENTER OF BOOKS FOR HANGING

Moveable Feast Table Runner & Napkins

A table runner and cloth napkins immediately turn eating into dining, and this combination is no exception. With a theme playing off Hemingway's *A Moveable Feast,* book covers of the 1920s Paris Lost Generation era are gathered into a fabric composition and accompanied by napkins printed with pages from the books. Look for editions of these classics with especially appealing covers. They can be hardcover or paperback, and because they are scanned, not cut apart, you can borrow them from your local library if you do not have them on your shelf.

For a list of Lost Generation authors, see page 130.

Seven books by Lost Generation
   authors (SEE LIST BELOW)

Printable fabric (SEE NOTE)

2 yards (2 m) cotton fabric
   (color/pattern of your choice)
   for the runner

Computer, scanner, and printer

Scissors

Straight pins

Sewing machine and thread

Iron

Bone folder

NOTE: *Most fabric and craft
stores sell printable fabric. Read the
manufacturer's instructions before
starting the project.*

LOST GENERATION AUTHORS

Sherwood Anderson

Djuna Barnes

Paul Bowles

Kay Boyle

H. D. (Hilda Doolittle)

John Dos Passos

Isadora Duncan

T. S. Eliot

F. Scott Fitzgerald

Janet Flaner

Ford Maddox Ford

Ernest Hemingway

Langston Hughes

Mary McCarthy

Henry Miller

Ezra Pound

Gertrude Stein

1 Print the fabric: For the table runner, scan all seven book covers and size them proportionately to fit an 8 ½ × 11" (A4) paper size, with the length set at 10" (25 cm). Be sure there is a minimum seam allowance of ½" (12 mm) along the sides.

   For the napkins, scan in four different book pages of your choice, choosing from the seven books, and size them proportionately to fit an 8½ × 11" (A4) paper size, with the length set at 10" (25 cm).

   Print all 11 images onto the printable fabric according to the package instructions. Peel the paper backing off each piece of printed fabric.

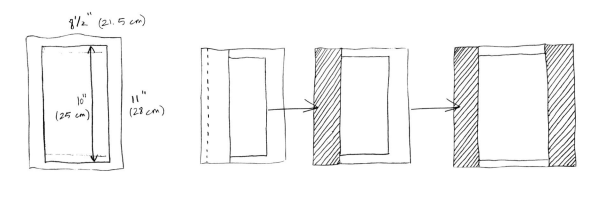

8½" (21.5 cm)

10"
(25 cm)

11"
(28 cm)

1   SCAN COVERS AND PRINT FABRIC

2   CONSTRUCT TABLE RUNNER FRONT BY
STITCHING FABRIC LENGTHS TO EITHER
SIDE OF BOOK COVERS

2 Construct the front of the table runner: Cut 8 pieces of runner fabric measuring 3 × 11" (7.5 × 28 cm) each. Then cut two pieces measuring 3 × 72" (7.5 × 180 cm). Decide upon the layout order of the book cover images.

Begin with the first book cover on the left of the layout; with right sides facing, align one of the 8 fabric lengths along the left edge of the cover image. Pin in place. Machine stitch with a ½" (12 mm) seam allowance. Press the seam open on the back.

Add a second fabric length to the right edge of the book cover image in the same way, pressing the seams open. Then stitch the second book cover image to

the fabric length and continue stitching the fabric lengths and book cover images together.

Once complete, align one of the 3 × 72" (7.5 × 180 cm) fabric lengths along one long edge of the stitched runner, with right sides facing. Pin the runner and fabric length together and trim any extra fabric at each short end. Machine stitch the layers together, using a ½" (12 mm) seam allowance, and press the seam open. Repeat with the second 3 × 72" (7.5 × 180 cm) fabric length, pinning and sewing it to the remaining long edge of the runner and pressing the seams open.

3 Back the table runner: Measure the length and width of the table runner and cut a piece of fabric to this size. With right sides facing, align all the edges and pin. Machine stitch the layers together, using a ½" (12 mm) seam allowance and leaving a 6" (15 cm) unstitched opening on one edge. Press all the seams with the iron and trim corners. Turn right side out through the opening and use the bone folder to get the corners pushed out completely; press all edges.

Topstitch in ¼" (6 mm) along all edges to close the opening and finish the edges.

4 Make the napkins: With the remaining fabric, cut four 8½ × 8½" (21.5 × 21.5 cm) pieces. With right sides facing, pin each page-printed fabric piece to the fabric. Machine stitch the layers together, using a ½" (12 mm) seam allowance and leaving a 4" (10 cm) unstitched opening on one edge. Press all seams open, trim the corners, and turn right side out. Use the bone folder to get the corners pushed out completely. Topstitch each napkin in ¼" (6 mm) along all edges to close the opening and finish the edges.

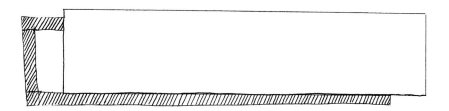

3   CUT BACKING AND STITCH TO TABLE RUNNER

NAPKINS

8½" (21.5 cm)

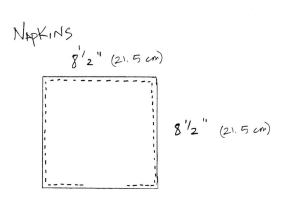

8½" (21.5 cm)

4   MAKE THE NAPKINS

Colophon Poster

MATERIALS

Colophon page or book
  with a colophon page

TOOLS

Computer and scanner

Thumb drive

Copy service provider
  (such as FedEx office)

Frame or binder clips and
  nails for hanging

A colophon is a page that contains publishing details, such a place and date of printing and often the publisher's mark, a logolike emblem. A classic mark is the Knopf borzoi dog. A book's colophon is found either on the back of the title page or at the very end of the book.

The idea of taking a minute and quiet detail and printing it larger than life as a poster so that it makes a statement is elegance at its purest. Embrace any wrinkles, creases, or other marks on your page as it gives the final print authenticity.

1 Scan the colophon at 300dpi. You can scan the image in black-and-white or color; the final image will print in black-and-white. Save the file to your desktop.

2 E-mail the file to a copy service provider. Alternatively, you can transfer it to a thumb drive and take it over.

3 Ask your copy service provider to print the image as a large-format black-and-white print. They will typically produce an image 36" (1 m) wide by any length. The print shown is 24 × 36" (60 cm × 1 m). I paid $5 for it.

4 To hang the colophon print, either frame it or simply attach two binder clips to either side of the top edge and slip the clips over nails in the wall.

Bookish Backdrop

MATERIALS

Books or book pages

TOOLS

Scanner

Computer with photoediting
software, such as Photo-
shop, and Internet access

It is easy to design your own book-themed wall-paper with one of the new custom printing companies such as Spoonflower. Books are an endless source of visuals, whether you choose to work with pages, covers, or, in my case here, old library pockets. Also consider using illustrated pages, title pages, or even book spines.

1 Choose a vendor to print your wallpaper and carefully review the user's guide. I used Spoonflower (www.spoonflower.com).

2 Scan each book element. Using your photoediting software, remove the backgrounds of all three files. Create a file size with a width that is a multiple of 24, (since the finished wallpaper is 24" [30 cm] wide) at 150 dpi. Set a ¼" (6 mm) margin on all sides. Drag and drop each of your book elements onto the page and begin your layout.

For my wallpaper, I scanned 21 different library pockets and set them into a simple grid on a document that is 24" (30 cm) wide.

(Keep in mind that if you are printing with Spoonflower, you have several repeat options, so consider these as part of your layout. Choose from basic, half-drop, half-brick, or mirror. You can also select the scale of the pattern with the size button.)

Choose a background color and add it to the file. Flatten all the layers (if using Photoshop) and save the file in a suitable format, such as JPG or TIFF.

3 Follow your vendor's guidelines for uploading and ordering the design. When the wallpaper arrives, install it according to the manufacturer's instructions.

RESOURCES

Below are the retailers from which I procured all of the supplies for the projects in this book.

ANTHROPOLOGIE
anthropologie.com
decorative drawer pulls
    and finials

BLICK ART
MATERIALS
dickblick.com
decorative paper
bookcloth
PVA glue
bone folder
linen hinging tape
bookboard

GAYLORD BROTHERS
gaylord.com
library supplies
library furniture and
    archival materials
library pockets
library borrower cards

HIROMI PAPER
hiromipaper.com
Kozo paper
bookcloth
bone folder
PVA glue
linen hinging tape

HOME DEPOT
homedepot.com
lumber
acrylic spray varnish

IKEA
ikea.com
basic home furnishings
    to reinvent
lazy Susan
Lack table
puck lights
towel bar

JO-ANN FABRIC AND
CRAFT STORE
joann.com
inkjet printable fabric

MICHAELS
michaels.com
Styrofoam balls
dowels
basswood strips

PAPER SOURCE
paper-source.com
cardstock
paper
envelopes

SPOONFLOWER
spoonflower.com
custom wallpaper
    and fabric

TALAS
talasonline.com
bookbinding leather
bookcloth
bone folder
PVA glue
linen hinging tape

TWILLTAPE.COM
twilltape.com
twill tape

MY FAVORITE BOOKS ON BOOKS

A Book of Books
Abelardo Morell

Book Was There
Andrew Piper

The Book as Art
Krystyna Wasserman,
Johanna Drucker, &
Audrey Niffenegger

Books: A Memoir
Larry McMurtry

The Care of Fine Books
Jane Greenfield

A Gentle Madness
Nicholas Basbane

Every Book Its Reader
Nicholas Basbane

Shakespeare and Company
Sylvia Beach

Libraries
Candida Höfer

*The Smithsonian Book
of Books*
Michael Olmert

*A History of Illuminated
Manuscripts*
Christopher De Hamel

MY FAVORITE BOOKSTORES

ARCANA BOOKS
More of a book*star* than a bookstore, Arcana is glamorous and well-respected. With tall stacks that you can silently graze among, it is like visiting a library specializing in art, film, fashion, architecture, and photography, except you can own these tomes. Display tables punctuate the aisles with featured titles. It was here that I got the idea for the Gallery Table on page 63.

arcanabooks.com
8675 Washington Blvd.
Culver City, CA 90232
310 458 1499

BART'S BOOKS
Like a lot of California structures, inside and outside are interwoven. At Bart's, books are grouped by subject in a warren of nooks and crannies where one minute you've got a roof over your head, the next minute, you're beneath the sun. Outside of the store there are several open bookshelves. When the store is closed you can buy a book from these and put your money (one dollar per book) in the box attached to the door. It is unhindered California-ness at its best.

bartsbooksojai.com
302 West Matlija St.
Ojai, CA 93023
805 646 3755

HARVARD BOOK STORE
This is an old haunt of mine. I remember going there mostly when the weather was inclement, running inside to where the books seemed to provide insulation from the damp and ice. Upstairs are the new, shiny, and pricey books. Downstairs are the used books. The beginnings of my art library came from here.

harvard.com
1256 Massachusetts Ave.
Cambridge, MA 02139
617 661 1515

MONOGRAPH BOOKWERKS
This judiciously curated bookshop is more of a destination than a store. An intimate bibliophilic paradise set inside a vintage Craftsman-style home, it has its focus on art, design, and photography books, old and new, small and large publishers.

monographbookwerks.com
5005 NE 27th Ave
Portland, OR 97211
503 284 5005

RIZZOLI BOOKSTORE
Barrel-vaulted, two-storied, and eruditely lit, this feels more like the private library of a collector than the retail site of a prestigious publisher. As it should, since they carry rare and collectible, antique, and foreign-language books. Walking through the wide-arched entrance recalls the occasion that going to a bookstore once was: an expedition into an alternate state.

rizzolibookstore.com
31 West 57th St.
New York, NY 10019
212 759 2424

SHAKESPEARE AND COMPANY
This is the bookshop of Sylvia Beach, who was no mere bookseller, but publisher of banned works, promoter of authors, ardent bibliophile, and den mother to Paris's creative community, receiving mail and providing a dry roof for many. During my Parisian summer I visited often, buying art books that I shipped home.

shakespeareandcompany.com
37, rue de la Bucherie
Paris, France
33 (0) 1 43 25 40 93

SMALL WORLD BOOKS
Tucked behind a bustling boardwalk café in Venice Beach is this bookshop for the reader, filled with the latest titles, underground classics, and local favorites. Stepping from the raucous and rumble of the strand into the serenity of the store is transformative. This is one of my favorite places to ride my bike to when I need a break.

smallworldbooks.com
1407 Ocean Front Walk
Venice, CA 90291
310 399 2360

ACKNOWLEDGMENTS

No book is created by one person alone, so I bestow my most gracious thanks to those who shared their time, skills, and prowess to help make this book. Thank you to Liana Allday for reaching out and planting the seed, to Lindsay Edgecombe for steadfastly guiding, and to Melanie Falick for orchestrating a grand finale.

Huge thanks to Gordon Hollis of Golden Legend Rare Books for leading me through the labyrinth that is book collecting, and sincerest gratitude to Wilfredo Chiesa and Tessa Gerling for lending the photos of *Relatos de un Paisaje Asesinado*.

Scores of thanks go to photographer Thayer Gowdy and stylist Karen Schaupeter for working with me on a second book to create the fresh and stunning images so vital to these pages.

And thanks to you holding this book, for a book is not complete without its reader.

ABOUT THE AUTHOR

Lisa Occhipinti is an exhibiting artist and writer. Her distinctive sculptures, embracing the physical form of the book, and photographs, based on books, are in private and corporate collections worldwide. She wrote and illustrated *The Repurposed Library* (STC Craft, 2011), which was featured in such publications as the *New York Times*, *Sydney Herald*, and *Irish Times* and by the Associated Press. This is her second book. She lives in Venice, California. Visit her at locchipinti.com

PUBLISHED IN 2014 BY STEWART, TABORI & CHANG
AN IMPRINT OF ABRAMS

LIBRARY OF CONGRESS CONTROL NUMBER: 2014930834

ISBN: 978-1-61769-087-7

EDITORS: LIANA ALLDAY AND MELANIE FALICK
DESIGNER: DEB WOOD
PATTERN DESIGNS ON PAGES 1, 2, 3, 5, 12, 13, 28, 29,
70, 71, 96, 97, 138, 139: SEBIT MIN AND DEB WOOD
PRODUCTION MANAGER: TINA CAMERON

THE TEXT OF THIS BOOK WAS COMPOSED IN LINOTYPE DIDOT,
SACKERS GOTHIC, AND MILLER TEXT.

PRINTED AND BOUND IN CHINA.
10 9 8 7 6 5 4 3 2 1

STEWART, TABORI & CHANG BOOKS ARE AVAILABLE AT
SPECIAL DISCOUNTS WHEN PURCHASED IN QUANTITY FOR
PREMIUMS AND PROMOTIONS AS WELL AS FUNDRAISING OR
EDUCATIONAL USE. SPECIAL EDITIONS CAN ALSO BE CREATED
TO SPECIFICATION. FOR DETAILS, CONTACT SPECIALSALES@
ABRAMSBOOKS.COM OR THE ADDRESS BELOW.

THE ART OF BOOKS SINCE 1949

115 WEST 18TH STREET
NEW YORK, NY 10011
WWW.ABRAMSBOOKS.COM